CORDELL CO~~UNTRY~~

By

Chris Bar~~ber~~

Discovering the Industrial Heritage of an ironmaking community
immortalized by Alexander Cordell's famous novel
"Rape of the Fair Country".

Cover Picture (Chris Barber)

Following Hill's tramroad past the Garnddyrys slag-heap.

First Published July 1985
2nd Impression November 1985

Copyright © Chris Barber
ISBN 0-9510444 0 0

Drawings and maps by Michael Blackmore

Technical advice by:—

Adrian Babbidge, John van Laun and
Michael Blackmore

*To the memory of my mother
who passed away in July 1984
and with thanks to my father
for his help and encouragement.*

BLORENGE
·BOOKS·

3, Holywell Road, Abergavenny, Gwent, NP7 5LP.
Tel: Abergavenny 3909

*Printed by Seargeant Brothers Printers Limited, Unit 9, Pontyfelin Road
Industrial Estate, New Inn, Pontypool, Gwent. NP4 0DQ.*

Hill's tramroad above Pwll-du Quarry contouring around the hillside to the site of Garnddyrys Ironworks.   *Chris Barber.*

CONTENTS

Acknowledgments

Foreword

Introduction

ACKNOWLEDGEMENTS

I would like to thank everyone who has helped me in the production of this book. In particular I thank Alexander Cordell for providing the inspiration and writing a foreword. Also I am greatly indebted to Michael Blackmore who shared my enthusiasm for the project and spent considerable time producing the drawings and maps to illustrate the scenes and features mentioned in the text. Mike and I spent fascinating hours discussing the detailed requirements for the artwork and his very special talent and extensive knowledge of the subject made him the ideal artist to do this work. I am grateful also to Francis Keen of Blaenafon for allowing me to make use of his fascinating collection of old photographs.

My thanks are also due to Victor Gollancz who first published Rape of the Fair Country (in 1959) for allowing me to include a number of quotations in this publication.

Rape of the Fair Country has sold millions of copies. It has been in print for over 25 years and has been published in seventeen languages. It has also been serialised on radio, the film rights have been sold and there are plans for the story to be televised.

To my father Bill Barber and several friends who helped me in a variety of ways, checking and making comments on my draft manuscript I am also very grateful.

With the permission of Alexander Cordell I have been able to include a number of extracts from a document he compiled in 1957 entitled "Pages from the Past" which was prepared as an entry for a local history competition sponsored by the South Wales Argus.

PLEASE NOTE.

All the routes described in this book are undertaken at the individual's own risk. The author or publisher cannot be held responsible for any accidents. Sensible footwear and waterproofs are advisable for the hill walking involved in following these routes. Walkers are also advised to use this guide book in conjunction with Ordnance Survey Map Sheet 161, 1:50,000 (Abergavenny and the Black Mountains). Sheet SO 21/31, 1:25,000 (Abergavenny) is also recommended.

Spelling of Garnddyrys.
Generally, I have utilised the Ordnance Survey spelling shown on the 1:50,000 map (Sheet 161) in the route descriptions. In his novel Rape of the Fair Country, Mr. Cordell uses the spelling **Garndyrus,** so this spelling occurs in several of the quotations.

FOREWORD

In 1954 I unloaded on to an unsuspecting public my first novel, one which was supposed to set the Thames on fire. In fact it earned just one-and-sixpence less than the royalty advance of £75 paid to me by the unfortunate publisher.

My form of transport in those days was a pedal-assisted auto-cycle which took me daily from Llanellen village to my work as a Civil Servant. I set about trying to be a better Civil Servant, but failed because the writer's bug began to bite me again. And one winter's night saw me standing near the Old Victoria Inn wondering what bomb had hit this area. It was clear that something had violated this once fair country.

The Old Victoria Inn.   *Photograph by Alexander Cordell.*

A man came walking with a bicycle out of the cold moonlight and he said his name was Parry; that he was a local postman on his way to visit his sister. I asked him what had happened to the place he called Garndyrus.

"Jawch, mun — terrible things have happened up here, don't you know?" I said I didn't, and Mr. Parry suggested that I should meet him the next evening at The Rolling Mill, a pub in Blaenafon. Next evening I was there at the appointed time, but Mr. Parry did not come. Some colliers, wondering at the stranger in their midst, engaged me in conversation: it isn't that the Welsh are nosey, they only want to know what's happening. I told them I was waiting for Mr. Parry, the postman.

"Duw", exclaimed a collier, "haven't you heard, mun? He died last night on his way to see his sister".

And so began scores of interviews with the old people whose tales of Blaenafon's past breathed life into Rape of the Fair Country. I wrote the book at white heat, scarcely altering a chapter: in between spells of writing I studied at the University of Wales, Aberystwyth and befriended every available librarian; more, I suddenly discovered that hand in hand with the tale of this mountain town went the last bloody revolution in Britain, the Chartist Rebellion, when men like John Frost a hundred years before their time, fought and suffered for the Six Point Charter — five of which we enjoy today in freedom.

Now thirty years later, my task as author of the book has long been ended, but Chris Barber, by introducing the solitary explorer or group to the paths and the lonely places where Iestyn Mortymer lived has done more than bring the story and its characters to life; he has succeeded in clothing an ancient skeleton with the flesh and blood of living history. Let the dry as dust historians bend us to their graphs and statistics, but it is given to creative people to hear the cry of a child trapped underground, or the sound of Welsh choirs echoing down the Sunday streets of a Welsh town. Myths and legends become living entities when a sixteen stone mountain fighter shivers when one mentions fairies. All the love and sacrifice that supported and upheld our forbears is reborn in the mind and heart of a solitary walker.

Cordell Country is more than a travelogue; it stands in a higher dimension, recapturing, as it does, the spirit and industry of a people who worked with fire; who raised dirt monuments to generations unborn; who travelled with specialist knowledge from Garndyrus and Blaenafon, to build the coke ovens of Philadelphia and the furnaces of Andrew Carnegie in Pitsburgh.

Go down into the valley of old Garndyrus and hold in your cupped hands the cinders of their long dead fires and they will tell you of themselves. . . Read this tale and you will hear the voices of these lost people calling on the wind . . you can, I assure you.

Alexander Cordell
Isle of Man.
February 1985.

INTRODUCTION

This walking guide was inspired by the historical novel "Rape of the Fair Country" by Alexander Cordell who has kindly written a foreword to these pages.

Cordell based his story on the iron forge of Garnddyrys where a small village on the western slopes of the Blorenge was inhabited by a hard working community whose lives for a period of about fifty years were linked with this almost forgotten industrial site.

The Mortymer family who are the main characters in the novel would have lived on the other side of the hill in Shepherd's Square near the Blaenafon Ironworks. From there it was just a short walk to the crest of the Turnpike road where one can look down into the valley of the Usk. A track led down from here to the Garnddyrys Forge and Rolling Mill where Hywel and Iestyn Mortymer worked twelve hours a day for six days a week. Iestyn started work there at the age of eight which was later than many of the children of that time. His father Hywel was a forge expert on the books of Crawshay Bailey the Nantyglo ironmaster and on loan to Garnddyrys.

Iestyn's sister, Morfydd scrubbed floors at the Manager's House in Nantyglo in the mornings and worked afternoons and evenings down the Coity Pit. *"They thought a lot of Morfydd in Nanty . . for she had quick fingers with bleeding when the children were caught in the trams, and she could deliver a baby underground as well as any doctor".*

For a number of years I have lived at Llanfoist, beneath the looming bulk of the Blorenge and on my regular walks across these fern clad slopes I find myself imagining Cordell's characters walking these same paths. I picture the hillside scarred by industry and imagine the sounds of horse-drawn trams, the roar of the furnaces and the whine of the rolling mill at Garnddyrys.

"The mountain was shuddering to the forge hammers of Garndyrus, and faintly on the wind came the plaintive singing of the Irish haulers. Llanfoist farms were sleeping in the pit-blackness below, their blind windows winking at the stars, and Abergavenny was a town of dead, strangled by the ribbon of the Usk that gleamed and flashed in the scudding moonlight".

Such is the descriptive power of Alexander Cordell. Read 'Rape of the Fair Country" (Coronet Books) for yourself and you also will be able to appreciate and visualise the historical and romantic associations of these locations.

Stand by the Balance Pond near Pwll-du and imagine young Iestyn Mortymer having a scrap with Moesen Jenkins for *"fighting by the Balance Pond was the custom and everything there being convenient for bruising: near home in case a man had to be carried, a gallows head with an oil lamp on it so you could see who you were hitting; and three feet of mud for the loser".*

Visit Llanfoist Wharf and conjure up a picture of the Garnddyrys village annual outing descending in trams down the steep inclines on the front of the Blorenge.

A hundred laughing people piling into the canal barges for their June outing to Newport Fair. *"The Garndyrus Benefit band was there; furnace-men, colliers, quarrymen and limestone carriers in Sunday suits with their wives and children adorned in best dresses and lace, even if it meant going twice into debt at the shop."*

Ascend the steep incline to reach Hill's tramroad contoured around the western slopes of the Blorenge and discover for yourself the site of the Garnddyrys Forge or the ruins of the village. Picture the women hanging out their washing, scrubbing their front steps whilst men stand smoking their clay pipes in doorways and children play "tag" in the street.

Make your way past Pen-fford-goch pond to reach the ruins of Blaenafon Ironworks and the workers' houses in Stack Square, Nearby was North Street where the Company Shop was located next door to the infamous Drum and Monkey inn. Cordell writes.

"The masters always paid out in the beer-houses. . .for the beer-houses were owned by the masters, too, and their paymasters always arrived late so that a man could drink on credit for hours before getting paid, and then be too drunk to count it."

Follow the road to Brynmawr and head for Nantyglo where the mighty ironworks of the Crawshay Bailey empire once stood. *". . .tall brick chimneys where the fire shot smoke poured and the mountain "trembled to the drop-hammers".*

In the same location, gaze up at the round towers built by the Bailey brothers, fortified and stocked with food to shelter them and their families when the men from their own works threatened to rise against them, plus the ruins of a private barracks for 'volunteers' - pro - employer workmen.

". . . the house of Bailey with its round battlements of stone. Beautiful was the garden, a splash of colour in the wilderness, facing square to the hovels of the labourers, and the thunder of the works."

Listen to the Redcoats marching in pairs from Brynmawr to Coalbrookvale and Nantyglo on a mission to keep the peace. On the mountains the Chartists are gathering for torchlight meetings to hear speeches from *"men like Henry Vincent who could sway a thousand men with a phrase and change the politics of women with a song."*

Think with sadness of the death of Hywel Mortymer - splashed by iron and half buried by bricks when a furnace split open and then wander across the moors of Mynydd Llangynidr and watch Iestyn Mortymer riding on a horse to a remote cave once used by the Chartists, where weapons were made and stored, *"pikeheads and spears that were to wrest power from the aristocracy and give it to the people."*

Finally, picture the scene described in the closing chapters of Cordell's story when thousands of men are marching down the Gwent valleys to overthrow the establishment and capture Newport. *"Men from Garnddyrys and Blaenafon, Coalbrookvale and Abertillery, Brynmawr and Nantyglo; wild men, starving men, soldiers with military bearing on the march to freedom."*

Chris Barber, Llanfoist, Abergavenny, Gwent, 1985.

HOW IT ALL BEGAN

Before the Industrial Revolution, Monmouthshire (now Gwent) remained a pastoral and agricultural area, with its small towns serving as local centres of trade and its population fairly evenly distributed.

An iron works, consisting of a small furnace and forge had been set up as early as 1565 at Pontypool by Capel Hanbury and there is also a record of a furnace being established at Blaenafon in 1600 but its location has yet to be discovered.

These early ironmasters used charcoal for fuel and water for power and accordingly their small ironworks were generally located in wooded valleys beside fast flowing streams near to supplies of iron ore. But as the wood became scarce they ran into problems.

'Many parts of this mountainous district, now wholly bare were covered formerly with large tracts of wood, charcoal being the only species of fuel originally used in the smelting, both in the bloomeries and in the furnaces.'

Archdeacon Coxe 1801.

In 1709 Abraham Darby of Coalbrookdale in Shropshire discovered that coal when used in the form of coke was a better fuel for smelting and the iron industry rapidly went into a new phase of development. Between 1760 and 1840 a chain of ironworks were established along a narrow strip of hill country stretching for about twenty miles between Blaenafon, (Monmouthshire) and Hirwaun (Glamorgan). Here there were rich deposits of ironstone, limestone and coal which were the essential materials required for the iron making process.

The first Ironmasters were from Staffordshire and the North of England and they exploited the mineral wealth of this area at the 'Heads of the Valleys' of South East Wales to make it the most important iron making region in Britain.

From this early industry where the only form of transport between the iron works and the coast was by packhorse, developed an urgent need for better communications, resulting in the construction of canals, tramroads and eventually railways. The valleys of Gwent and Glamorgan were rapidly converted from a land of wooded hillsides and sparkling clear rivers to one of the most concentrated areas of British industry. People seeking work came in their thousands from the rural areas of Wales, England and Ireland, attracted by the possibility of employment or higher wages.

Between 1801 and 1921 the population of Monmouthshire increased from 45,000 to 450,000. With the influx of so many immigrant workers into the area, English became the main language in the valleys of South Wales although many still locals firmly clung to their traditions and still brought up their children to speak Welsh.

Today, many areas of dereliction have been transformed by an extensive landscaping and tree planting programme which has made the valleys green again. The discovery of industrial remains and the study of living conditions in the hard times of 19th century Britain has caught the imagination of a very large number of people during the last two decades and South East Wales is one of the most rewarding and fascinating areas to explore.

The Blorenge and the five arches of Llanfoist Bridge.

The Blorenge.

"To the west (of Abergavenny) rises the Blorenge, magnificent from its height and continuity; it forms the northern extremity of the chain, which reaches from Pontypool, and terminates near the confines of the county. The highest part towers above the Usk and the town of Abergavenny; its sides are concave; the summit is covered with russet herbage, without a single bush; the midland parts are chequered with underwood, intermixed with fertile meadows, and the base is clothed with timber trees. At the northern extremity, the rich knoll of Upper Llanfoist presents a wood of fine oak, ash and elm, forming an extensive mantle of thick and dark foliage."

Archdeacon Coxe (1801)

The Blorenge is rendered interesting on many accounts. It forms a termination to the great mineral basin of South Wales, and it is situated on what was formerly termed "The Wilds of Monmouthshire". Here terminates the valley, Afon Llwyd, named from the stream running through it. From its bowels, the Blaenafon, the Garnddyrys and, in the same measure, the Nantyglo Iron Works, extract their wealth."

John White (1887).

12

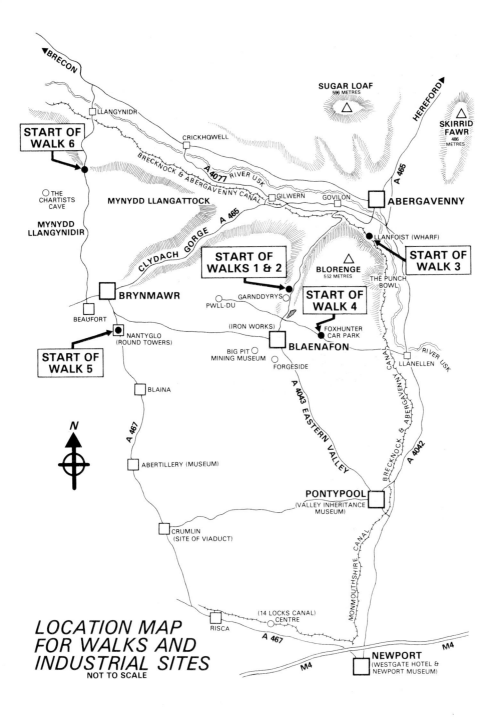

BRECON

SUGAR LOAF
596 METRES

HEREFORD

SKIRRID FAWR
486 METRES

LLANGYNIDR

CRICKHOWELL

START OF WALK 6

BRECKNOCK & ABERGAVENNY CANAL

A 4077 RIVER USK

GILWERN   GOVILON

ABERGAVENNY

A 465

THE CHARTISTS CAVE

MYNYDD LLANGATTOCK

MYNYDD LLANGYNIDR

A 465

CLYDACH GORGE

LLANFOIST (WHARF)

START OF WALK 3

START OF WALKS 1 & 2

BLORENGE
552 METRES

THE PUNCH BOWL

START OF WALK 4

GARNDDYRYS

PWLL-DU

BRYNMAWR

(IRON WORKS)

FOXHUNTER CAR PARK

BEAUFORT

NANTYGLO (ROUND TOWERS)

BIG PIT MINING MUSEUM

BLAENAFON

RIVER USK

LLANELLEN

START OF WALK 5

FORGESIDE

BLAINA

A 467

A 4043 EASTERN VALLEY

BRECKNOCK & ABERGAVENNY CANAL

A 4042

N

ABERTILLERY (MUSEUM)

PONTYPOOL
(VALLEY INHERITANCE MUSEUM)

CRUMLIN (SITE OF VIADUCT)

MONMOUTHSHIRE CANAL

(14 LOCKS CANAL) CENTRE

RISCA

A 467

M4

M4

NEWPORT
(WESTGATE HOTEL & NEWPORT MUSEUM)

LOCATION MAP FOR WALKS AND INDUSTRIAL SITES
NOT TO SCALE

WALK 1
Garnddyrys and Pwll-du. (3 hours)

Park on the west side of the B 4246, Blaenavon to Abergavenny road, near a footpath sign. (F.P Pwll-du 1.3 km) at Grid Reference SO 259122.

Follow a wide track passing a large oval hollow on the right. This is the site of a pond that once provided water power to the Garnddyrys Forge. The track zig zags down passing a lower pond site on the left, to join a fence. The views down into Cwm Llanwenarth are impressive. Turn a corner and ahead can be seen an enormous hunk of slag resembling a prehistoric monster. (See page 22 for continuation of route description).

The Garnddyrys Forge and Rolling Mill were only in operation for about half a century and only a comparatively small amount of information has come to light about its history. Many people might understandably wonder why a forge and rolling mill came to be established here in the first place. There were in fact three main reasons:—

(1) When the Brecknock and Abergavenny Canal was linked with the Monmouthshire Canal at Pontymoile near Pontypool in 1812 it was a condition by Act of Parliament that goods transported via the B&A were charged the same rate as on the Monmouthshire Canal. Accordingly the Blaenafon Company, by transporting goods around the hillside and down to Llanfoist could make a substantial reduction in their shipment costs to Newport.
By comparison the tolls on the Monmouthshire Canal via Pontnewynydd were excessive.

(2) Limestone, coal and ironstone were already being obtained from the Pwll-du side of the hill. This meant that trams could travel to a forge sited at Garnddyrys loaded with pig iron and then return via Pwll-du carrying coal and limestone.

(3) In addition coal and limestone could also be transported in the other direction via a steep incline to Llanfoist where an added attraction was the proposed tramroad to Llanfihangel. This would offer an opportunity for trade in the agricultural markets of Herefordshire. Coal and limestone could also be shipped up the canal to Brecon in one direction and the finished iron products from Garnddyrys could travel to Newport in the other. It was all a question of economics.

"Garndyrus standing at the head of the Eastern Valley above Blaenavon, became a thriving industrial centre with the advent of Messrs Hopkins, Hill and Pratt, who in 1782 leased 12,000 acres of land from the Marquis of Abergavenny for the comparatively small rental of £1300 annually.
Hopkins was a Blaenavon man, his two partners men of Staffordshire. All three were industrious and resourceful. They invested a total of £40,000 in richly wooded country, aware no doubt of its hidden wealth. But it is doubtful if they fully realised the extent of that wealth or that the land that they gained so cheaply would be yielding its treasures for over a hundred years after their deaths.

14

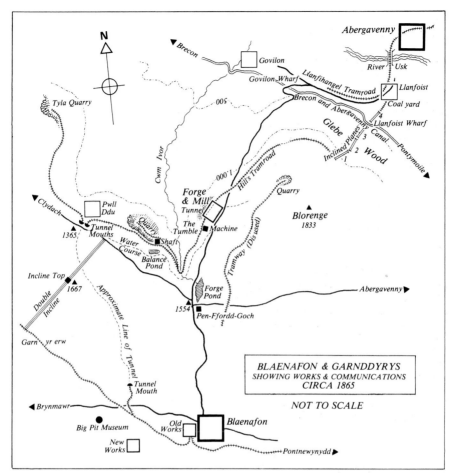

In the map:

N

Abergavenny

Brecon

Govilon

Govilon Wharf

River Usk

Llanfihangel Tramroad

Llanfoist

Brecon and Abergavenny Canal

Coal yard

Tyla Quarry

Llanfoist Wharf

Glebe

Inclined Planes

Wood

Pontymoile

Cwm Ivor

Hill's Tramroad

Forge & Mill

Quarry

Tunnel

Blorenge
1833

Pwll Ddu

Clydach

The Tumble

Machine

Tramway (Disused)

Tunnel Mouths
1365

Quarry

Shaft

Water Course

Balance Pond

Abergavenny

Incline Top
1667

Forge Pond

Double Incline

Approximate Line of Tunnel

1554

Pen-Ffordd-Goch

Garn yr erw

Tunnel Mouth

Brynmawr

BLAENAFON & GARNDDYRYS
SHOWING WORKS & COMMUNICATIONS
CIRCA 1865

NOT TO SCALE

Big Pit Museum

Old Works

Blaenafon

New Works

Pontnewynydd

In the year of the French Revolution, their first furnace began to operate at Garndyrus. Four others followed in quick succession, and a bare mountainside with its usual quota of farm holdings became an industrial area destined to play a major role in the wealth of Wales.

But great difficulties of transport prevailed, for the finished iron had to be sent by pack mule across mountain tracks to Newport for export. An extension of the Newport canal to Abergavenny in 1806 eased the problem, and after this date, Garndyrus iron was transported by horse - tram around the breast of the Blorenge mountain. From the bowl of the mountain it was dropped down the incline, an ingenious system of counter balancing being employed, to the canal wharf at Llanfoist, whence it was transported by barge to Newport thus cutting the distance to the docks by half."

Alexander Cordell
Pages from the Past 1957.

15

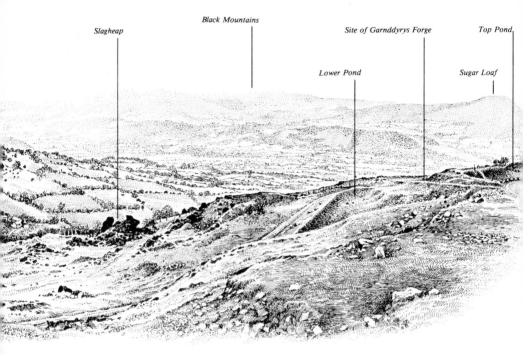

Slagheap   Black Mountains   Site of Garnddyrys Forge   Top Pond

Lower Pond   Sugar Loaf

The site of Garnddyrys Iron Forge above Cwm Llanwenarth.

Situated at an altitude of 1,300 feet this site is a most unlikely one for an industrial undertaking and one may wonder at the daring and enterprise of the men who were responsible for such an endeavour. The land for the forge site was purchased in 1817 from William Price for £75 and the following year the long strip of land for Hill's tramroad from Garnddyrys to Llanfoist was acquired from John Hanbury Williams.

This little hillside forge turned out some 300 tons of finished product in a week's operation. Iron bars and rails were produced which were transported to many parts of Britain and to various countries throughout the world. Horse shoes were also made here for the horses that worked for the Blaenavon Company.

The Ponds

The two ponds which are now dry were each approximately one acre in area and they were constructed to supply water to the steam engines which were in use on the site. An outlet can be seen in the retaining wall of the upper pond. This was the supply point to the workings below. Unfortunately it was found that these two ponds were not large enough to supply sufficient water to efficiently operate both the forge and the mill so another pond was constructed at Penfford goch to provide additional water. A water channel may also be seen contouring around the hillside carrying water from the old coal levels at Pwll du to top up the Garnddyrys ponds.

16

The Worker's Houses

Most of the workers who operated this site could practically fall out of bed into work, so conveniently situated were their houses. The nearest dwellings were in the Garnddyrys Square which consisted of 20 houses built on three sides of a rectangle providing 5, 10 and 5 houses on each side. By 1870 these had already been partly demolished.

A separate block known as Garnddyrys Row consisted of 15 houses in one block. They are clearly shown on the 1827 one inch to the mile scale Ordnance map, and by 1938 they were abandoned.

Another block was appropriately known as 'Ten Houses' and nearby were 'Pond Houses' which provided fourteen dwellings in two blocks of 6 and 8. They were probably built in about 1830. The families living on this site were largely Welsh but many came from Staffordshire and Ireland.

The Tunnel (SO 258119)

An interesting feature that can be examined on the site is a short tunnel which was probably constructed to protect the tramroad from slag. It is about 6 foot 6 inches high, 8 feet 6 inches wide and the total length was about 150 yards. There is a section of about 35 yards that can be entered with care.

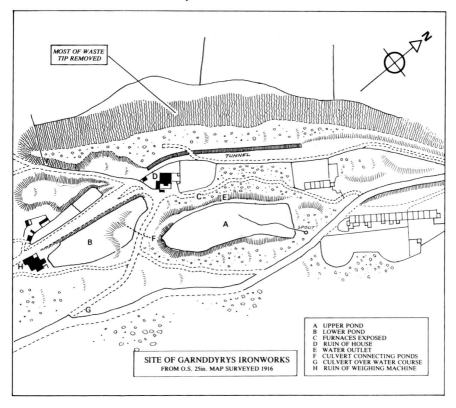

MOST OF WASTE TIP REMOVED

TUNNEL

SPOUT

D

C   E

A

B

F

H

G

SITE OF GARNDDYRYS IRONWORKS
FROM O.S. 25in. MAP SURVEYED 1916

A   UPPER POND
B   LOWER POND
C   FURNACES EXPOSED
D   RUIN OF HOUSE
E   WATER OUTLET
F   CULVERT CONNECTING PONDS
G   CULVERT OVER WATER COURSE
H   RUIN OF WEIGHING MACHINE

Water outlet in the western retaining wall of the Upper Pond. This was the supply point to the workings below.

The Slag Heap
Looking like a prehistoric monster this was the main slag dump. There is a circular access road to it.

18

Garnddyrys Iron Forge in 1820

This rough sketch drawn by Sir Richard Colt Hoare is the only known illustration of the Garnddyrys Forge. He made this drawing whilst standing on Hill's Tramroad at Pwll-du quarries and it shows the forge as it existed in about 1820. The sketch only came to light in 1984 and it was discovered by John van Laun.

It was an exciting find that provided the basis for Michael Blackmore to produce a re-construction drawing of the Garnddyrys Forge showing its exact location, the tracks tramroads and the workers' houses located at the area on the hillside known as 'The Tumble'.

A re-construction of Garnddyrys Forge, immortalised by Alexander Cordell and now brought to life through the pen of Mike Blackmore. This is how it may have looked in about 1850. Billowing smoke rises from the tall chimneys of the puddling furnaces where the pig iron was converted into wrought iron and a rolling mill produced the final products such as bars, rails and plates. It is of interest that the iron for Crumlin viaduct was produced here in the 1850's.

The following is an extract from the minutes book giving an account of a shareholders meeting held on 22nd April 1853 to decide the fate of the Garnddyrys Forge.

"The Works having now returned to a profitable condition the Directors have again seriously considered the best means of increasing the production of wrought iron, and at the same time of still further diminishing the expense of its manufacture. They are satisfied that this may be accomplished by the removal of the mill from Garnddyrys and its re-erection, with increased power and efficiency, on the Freehold Property of the Company at Blaenafon, and they desire to call the attention of the shareholders to their reasons for this conviction.

"The site of the mill at Garnddyrys has been a constant cause of inconvenience and expense on account of its distance from the H.Q. at Blaenavon, and now that the Monmouthshire Canal Company have reduced their tonnages and improved the mode of conveyance along their road, these disadvantages are the more strikingly felt; the transit from Garnddyrys being by a circuitous and expensive route of twenty four miles, while the port of Newport will be reached by a locomotive railway from Blaenavon of only 16 miles.

"The power of the present mill is scarcely equal to the production of 200 tons per week, it is proposed to make the new one, eventually, more than double that power say equal to 500 tons per week, this increase, while tending to reduce the cost of the common charges upon each ton made, will enable the company to enter more largely into the manufacture of rails, and to add that of 'tyre Iron' and 'Boiler Plates' two articles for which the Blaenavon iron is believed to be peculiarly well adapted.

"Taking all these points into consideration the Directors have commenced this important alteration, as the means not only of increasing very materially the profit of the concern in favourable times, but what is of equally essential importance, of saving the company from losses in unfavourable years."

In 1860 the plant was dismantled and the rolling mill was incorporated into a new works erected on the Coity side of Blaenafon at Forgeside.

Walk around the hunk of slag and follow the track downhill, ignoring any tracks on the right or left, to reach a metal gate. Go through and pass below the remains of a stone cottage; its open doorway offering a basement shelter for damp sheep. The track leads down across a stream and through the fields. Look up to your right to see other ruined cottages that were once part of Garnddyrys village.

The census of 1851 shows that some 300 people lived near the Garnddyrys Forge.

After heavy rain the streams chatter noisily in the valley below and squirrels may often be seen shinning along branches overhead. Pass through a gate by Blaen-y-cwm farm and turn left down the drive. On reaching a road go straight

across to follow a grass lane between stone walls to reach a neat footbridge over a rushing stream. Then on between hedges, past a barn to reach a gate. Cross another stream and follow a path ascending diagonally to the right between tumbled stone walls. Through the trees on the right can be seen Ysgyryd Fawr, a sinister looking hill.

In due course the track curves back to the left and steepens, now following an old incline leading up to the quarries on the hillside above. An unrelenting slope that may make the unfit puff and gasp a little. But at last the gradient levels out and the reward is a fine view across Cwm Llanwenarth. Directly opposite can be seen Garnddyrys and above is your vehicle seemingly stuck with superglue to the hillside.

Continue along the track below some limestone quarries to shortly reach a metal gate. Go through and the track ascends gently to bend right by another gate in a stone wall. Head up to meet an old tram road and follow it to the left. (Just below and parrallel to a gravel track) to reach a metal stile in a stone wall. This stile is unusual being constructed from old rails and girders and looks as if it should last for many years to come. Continue beside a hedge and then through a gate. Soon you will see a low archway on the right. This is the entrance to the Pwll-du tunnel which was constructed to connect the Blaenavon Iron Works with Garnddyrys Forge and was opened in about 1822. The tunnel was nearly one and a half miles long and the men who led the horse drawn trams through it must have cursed this subterranean route for it was then the longest tramroad tunnel in Britain.

North Portal of the Pwll-du tram road tunnel. (SO 246116)

23

Pwll-du Tunnel

This 1½ mile tunnel was constructed for the purpose of transporting coal and limestone from Pwll-du to be used in the Blaenafon Iron Works. When the Garnddyrys forge came into operation it meant that on the outward journey the empty trams could be loaded with pig iron thus making its use dual purpose. Unfortunately the route was single track and it became very congested, causing much wasted time, effort and no doubt frequent accidents must have occurred. So in due course a double incline was constructed over the top. (See walk 4).

The Blaenafon side of the tunnel had an impressive entrance which was referred to as the Marble Arch. (SO 248098)

It is interesting that Archdeacon Coxe in 1801 (Coxe's Tours in Monmouthshire) referred to a mine level worked by the Blaenavon Ironworks Company that went for 3/4 mile into the hill. This level was probably utilised when the Pwll-du tunnel was constructed.

When the last horse finished work in the tunnel it was apparently shot and buried in full harness.

The building across to the left is the old village hall of Pwll-du and it is one of the few remaining buildings of this once thriving village. It is now used as an Adventure Centre. There were once two ranks of houses in this village — upper rank and lower rank with 14 and 28 houses respectively.

One of the Pwll-du pubs used to be the Prince of Wales where one bar was situated in Monmouthshire and the other in Breconshire, thus making it possible to have a drink on the same day in two counties in the same pub! At one time this pub was used as the company shop.

On joining the Pwll-du road turn left and shortly take a gravel track on the left. Go down to the right of a white cottage (once the Lamb Inn) and through a wooden gate to follow a narrow track between a fence and a stone wall to a gate. Keeping left of a small pond go through a third gate and then turn right to follow a track leading around the hillside to a narrow cutting. Follow the right bank above the cutting. (N.B. Do not enter the cave below as the roof is unstable and very dangerous).

Just before a stream, descend steeply with care and go over a stile to follow a stone wall on the left. Look across to the left to see the top of the balance shaft of Pwll-du quarry. The water supply that operated this ingenious lifting system was supplied from a reservoir on the hillside above. (SO 253113)

Hill's well engineered tramroad contours around the head of Cwm Ifor providing impressive views. If you have young children with you take care here. . . for there is a steep drop on the left. Soon you cross a stream and the tramroad heads directly back to Garnddyrys. The slag "monster" can be seen ahead and your car awaits you on the hillside above.

"The Garndyrus furnaces are silent now; mere skeletons of greatness that nature by constant effort, is striving to obliterate. And it is difficult to believe, as one stands today on the crest of the Keeper's road that this was once a thriving community, a little town of people who lived their lives on the edge of a golden valley, who laughed and cried and brought forth children; who made iron of a quality incomparable; who sent their sons abroad to teach the art; whose sister town of Blaenafon sent her sons to Staffordshire to build new ovens, and as far abroad as Philadelphia to tell them there, as Betsy Williams, Blaenavon born, old and wise, once told her masters how to make good iron.

Garndyrus is gone, but the canal still stands as a tribute to her greatness; down which poured the thousands of tons that served the world."

Alexander Cordell
'Pages from the Past' 1957.

Abergavenny with the River Usk in the foreground. 19th Century Engraving.

Abergavenny
Abergavenny must have been a very pleasant place for the industrial workers from Blaenavon and Garnddyrys to visit, particularly on market days. They no doubt let off steam and upset the local people who looked with much disfavour on these rough people from the 'top towns'. The Garnddyrys families went to church in St. Mary's on Sundays and on market days the men put away their quarts of ale in the Fountain Inn which used to stand on the present day site of Richard's the Ironmongers. On the return journey they may have paused at the Gardners' Arms, The Wharf, Troed y Rhiw, the Puddlers' Arms or the Royal Oak before reaching the Victoria ('Queens') at Garnddyrys for a final drink to quench their thirst after the long ascent from Abergavenny.

WALK 2
Pwll-du Quarries (2½ hours)

This route starts from the same location as Walk 1 on the B 4246 above Garnddyrys. (SO 259122)

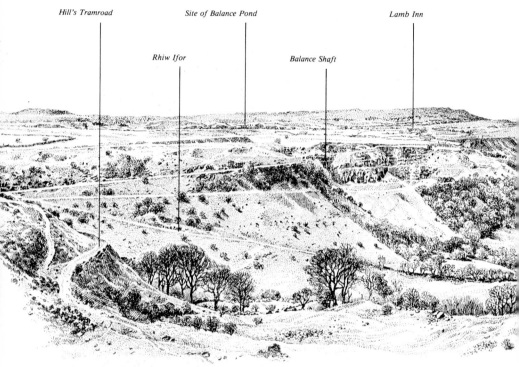

Hill's Tramroad   Site of Balance Pond   Lamb Inn

Rhiw Ifor   Balance Shaft

The head of Cwm Llanwenarth showing Hill's Tramroad and Pwll-du Quarry.

Follow the track down overlooking the site of the upper pond. Leave the main track and follow a path down to the left of the wooden pylons and descend beside the remains of an old stone wall to join Hill's tram road. Turning left, follow the tram road around to the head of the valley and cross the stream at the head of Cwm Ifor. On reaching a junction of tracks, follow a path descending to the right for about twenty yards and then take a narrow track on the left, maintaining height. This track is parallel to Hill's tram road and it crosses the hillside below a line of cliffs. Go across a stile and traverse around the steep slope to reach Pwll-du Quarry. A stream tumbles down the hillside on the left. Just to the right of this stream at ground level is a low entrance to a cave. It is interesting to squirm inside to enter a small chamber and then pass through a hole into a wide man made verticle shaft. (Balance Shaft SO 251115). stretching skywards. It forms a fantastic echo chamber if you feel inclined to burst into song!

26

This shaft was cut through the limestone to enable a water balance lifting system to be installed which was used to raise loaded trams to a higher level. The water utilised to operate the system came from the Balance Pond higher up, (SO 253113).

Line of tramroad

Balance shaft

Pwll-du Quarry showing the top of the Balance Shaft. Chris Barber 1983.

A large wheel fitted with a powerful brake was fixed above the top of the pit. It had a rope or a chain passing around it. To one end an empty cistern was attached which carried over it a tram of limestone. The other end of the chain was attached to a cistern which when filled with water was heavier than the loaded tram and the empty cistern combined.

The cistern was filled from a tank nearby and a brake regulated its descent. When it reached the bottom of the shaft a self acting valve would release the water which either escaped to the surface by an addit or was drawn up by a pump. The loaded tram was removed from the empty cistern which was then filled with water. Then the cistern at the bottom of the shaft was emptied and a tram placed on it and so on. . .

A group of quarry workers pictured near Pwll-du in 1890, picture supplied by Francis Keen.

Quarry workers at Pwll-du provided the limestone that was used in the iron making process at Blaenafon. Their work was hard and dangerous and accidents were frequent. Excess limestone (and coal) was sent to Herefordshire and Breconshire for the farms.

On leaving the cave go down a narrow cutting opposite to reach the edge of the escarpment and walk around to the left following a path overlooking Cwm Llanwenarth. Head for some hawthorn trees where a path winds around the edge of the slope to pass an iron boundary marker. Continue towards a television mast directly ahead. The path rises a little and then descends to join a path flanked by a post and rail fence. Turn right and follow this path with its metal hand rail down into the valley to reach a metal gate. Continue across a field into a picturesque valley and a tumbling stream. Then on to a stone barn and go right over a stone bridge to follow a track down to a tarmac road. Turn right through a gate and up the drive to Blaen-y-cwm farm. Take the second gate on the right opposite a barn and follow the path up through the fields to reach a gate near a ruined cottage. Then bearing left carry on up a wide track to the site of Garnddyrys Forge and your starting point.

WALK 3
Circuit of the Blorenge (4-5 hours)

Start from Llanfoist village for the complete walk. But if you wish to leave out the steep ascent of the Llanfoist Inclines, drive up the B 4246 and start in the same location as Walks 1 & 2. (See pages 14 and 37 for route descriptions).

Please note. If you wish to park at the Llanfoist Inn permission must be obtained first.

From Llanfoist walk towards Govilon and about 100 yards past the inn turn left up a lane beside the little church of St. Faith (Ffwyst). Go over a stone stile on the left if you wish to see the grave of Crawshay Bailey. It is in the left hand corner of the churchyard where you will find a tall marble pillar appropriately surrounded by sturdy iron railings.

Crawshay Bailey was the nephew of Richard Crawshay who came from Yorkshire and leased the Cyfarthfa ironworks at Merthyr in 1786. By 1794 he was able to buy the works and his wealth increased rapidly. His young nephew Crawshay Bailey arrived in Merthyr to learn the iron trade in the employment of his uncle. In a short time Crawshay Bailey made rapid progress to become one of the chief industrialists in Monmouthshire. He constructed railways, sank pits and was involved in the construction of canals in addition to developing one of the world's largest ironworks at Nantyglo.

In later years he also turned to politics and became Member of Parliament for Monmouthshire and Newport Borough. Crawshay Bailey will always be remembered for his railway schemes and his memory is perpetuated by a song with numerous verses — unprintable and otherwise which tells of his amazing engine.

> *Crawshay Bailey had an engine*
> *And he found it wouldn't go*
> *So he pulled it by a string,*
> *All the way to Nantyglo.*

Chorus:
> *Did you ever see,*
> *Did you ever see,*
> *Did you ever see,*
> *Such a funny thing before?*

> *Crawshay Bailey had an engine,*
> *She was a puffin' and a-steamin',*
> *And accordin' to her power,*
> *She could do four miles an hour.*
> *Chorus: Did you ever see etc.*

Crawshay Bailey an avid freemason, worked hard for nearly 75 years and is probably the most famous of all the ironmasters. On his retirement he lived in Llanfoist House and he was 83 years old when he passed away.

29

Crawshay Bailey

"His death cast a gloom over the whole district, although his length of years had been extended beyond nature's limit. No man assisted more to develop the resources of the mineral districts of Monmouthshire and Glamorganshire than did the deceased gentleman; and up to the last half dozen years he pursued the active life he had been accustomed to follow from his youthful days.

He was elected representative in Parliament for the united boroughs of Monmouth, Newport and Usk in 1852 and resigned his seat in 1868. He peacefully expired on Tuesday January 9th 1872 at his residence Llanfoist House.

Some years before his death Mr. Bailey purchased Llanfoist House, in the neighbourhood of Abergavenny where he resided in retirement since the disposal of the works. A short time before his death he undertook at his own expense to provide a clock for the tower of Abergavenny new market hall, which unfortunately he did not live to see completed. A still greater boom conferred by him upon Abergavenny was the interest he took in promoting the making of the Merthyr, Tredegar and Abergavenny Railway.

Mr. Crawshay Bailey came of a Yorkshire family of respectable position, though of ordinary circumstances. His father married a Miss Crawshay, sister to the founder of the Cyfarthfa works.

The mortal remains of the Iron King (an appellation by which the deceased gentleman was familiarly known at the seats of his manufacturing operations) were deposited in their last resting place at Llanfoist."

Usk Gleaner 1878.

30

Two stained glass windows in Llanfoist church (which his son restored) serve as a memorial to him.

Few people realise it now but in this same quiet graveyard in an unmarked grave lies Samuel Baldwyn who made a very important contribution to the development of the iron industry in the 19th century. Born in Chepstow in 1778 Samuel as a young man set up a printing and bookselling business there. However, he later went to Pontypool to live and having developed a strong interest in science he took a job in a laboratory there. In due course he became a remarkable research chemist and was the first man to refine pig iron with a basic slag on a limestone bottom. He also became famous in his day as the inventor of the iron — bottomed puddling furnace which raised the weekly output of a furnace from 8 tons to 20 tons approximately.

It was also Samuel Baldwyn who was the first to recognise that the Newport area was an ideal location for a giant iron or steel works and he advanced this idea in a paper published in 1859 — recommending Llanwern as a suitable location. (102 years later work commenced on the giant Spencer works at Llanwern). He also drew up plans for a Severn Bridge nearly 100 years before it was built. This quiet inventive man died in 1863 and was buried here at Llanfoist. A genius ahead of his time unhonoured and forgotten.

The Llanfoist tunnel beneath the Brecknock and Abergavenny Canal.

31

Continuing up the lane go right where it bends to the left and follow a path through a tunnel beneath the canal. It is an eerie experience to tramp through this stone-lined passage with the noise of your feet echoing off the walls and mixing with the sound of a gurgling stream which flows into a gulley (once called the Devil's Gulley) on one side of the tunnel. The tunnel was built to allow the old parish road to pass under the canal. It is 40 yards long and approximately 6' wide and 7' high — but most people will automatically duck their heads.

Constructed for pedestrian use this route was no doubt used daily by men who lived in Llanfoist and worked on the incline on the hillside above.

Above the tunnel is the old Wharfmaster's House and nearby is the Hill's Warehouse, locally known as the boathouse. This was once a bustling scene of industrial activity where the trams from Garnddyrys were unloaded for shipment of iron and coal to Newport Docks and limestone to Brecon and Hereford.

Imagine the scene here as Iestyn Mortymer and the people of Garnddyrys return from their annual outing to Newport Fair.

"Listen! Otters are barking along the Usk. The June moon is flashing and the arched bridges step over us all the way from Ponty. Faint is the singing of the night-shift Irish as the home coming barges drift under the shadow of the mountain. The barge men are astir, yawning and stretching. Women begin their chattering, tired children their crying. Ropes are coiled for flinging, windlasses turn in shrieks as Llanfoist Wharf comes flaring through the mist. To the hostile stares of the Irish who pelted us, we help our women out and into the trams for the climb to Garndyrus."

On emerging from the tunnel, go straight ahead to ascend the Llanfoist incline steeply up through the woods and beside a stream. The incline was constructed in three stages. The top section was 1 in 3 and about 270 yards in length. Stage 2 fell 225 feet in about 300 yards and the final section fell 300 feet in 350 yards. Between each incline was a platform where a brake wheel was sited and here the trams had to be transferred to the next stage.

The Inclines
A winch house was situated high up in the Blorenge Bowl (SO 277127). The trams descended to a collecting area (just above the present tree level) where the loads were re-sorted and the trams arranged in order of priority before being sent down the second stage of the incline which was known as "The Big Drop". Full trams descended under gravity pulling empty ones up on the other track. Accidents were frequent, often caused by badly loaded and runaway trams.

Spanish ore of high quality (70% — Blorenge ore was only 26%) was shipped from Newport by barge to Llanfoist and then sent up the incline to Garnddyrys to pass through the Pwll-du tunnel to Blaenavon. It later returned through the tunnel as pig iron en route for Garnddyrys for the next stage in the process to finally descend the incline as a finished product.

As you climb up the incline look out for stones with holes bored into them where the double line of rails was once secured. Unfortunately, very few of the stones are still in position for they have been knocked aside by motorbikes and tumbled into the stream by vandals lacking an appreciaton of their historical importance.

A brakewheel was set in a pit to control the descent of the trams down the incline. Passing around the brake wheel was a continuous chain or rope which was fastened to the trams on each line of rails.

Grooves cut by the passage of the chain or rope may be observed on certain stones still in place on the incline.

Looking down the Llanfoist Incline

Thankfully, you reach a platform at the end of the first incline which provides an opportunity to catch your breath. This is a steep ascent at the start of any walk.

Continue up past a little brick hut and tall beech trees to reach a stile. Further on you will emerge from the woods, high on the hollow of Cwm Craf. The final section of incline went up at an angle to the right at this point.

Keep going straight up to meet a stile. Pause and look back now for Abergavenny is spread out below you and the view takes in the Sugar Loaf, and Skirrid Fawr, Graig Syfryddin and Skirrid Fach.

Go over the stile and head up beside a fence. At its highest point ignore the route ascending the steep slope above and go to the right aiming for the edge of a stone wall directly ahead. Then continue along the tramroad which becomes well defined at this point. This is Hill's tramroad and it was constructed in about 1820. It ran from the mouth of the Pwll-du tunnel to Garnddyrys Forge and then followed the 1200′ contour line to the front of the Blorenge where it connected with the three inclined planes descending to Llanfoist Wharf. This route as a tramroad became redundant in about 1865 after the closure of the Garnddyrys Forge.

Hill's Tramroad on the north slope of the Blorenge near the top of the Llanfoist Incline. (SO 246116—SO 284131)

34

Thomas Evan Watkins who wrote a short history of Llanfoist in 1834 provided the following description of Hill's Tramroad and the Llanfoist inclines.

"The tramroad runs almost evenly with the edge of the Blorenge to the side of Cwm craf, where pulleys, wheels and iron chains liberate the trams loaded with coal, iron and limestone down the terrible slope to their first resting situation, where a similar apparatus dispatches them onwards to the second stage, and then another to the third on the Brecon and Abergavenny canal bank, and likewise the loaded trams bring the empty ones up the steep heights on the side of Cwm craf to the canal. Here they unload the trams and fill the boats with iron etc for the port of Newport-on-Usk to meet the ships which sail from pole to pole to all the harbours of the habitable globe."

Continuing around the northern slopes of the Blorenge you can enjoy a bird's eye view of Abergavenny and the Vale of Usk.

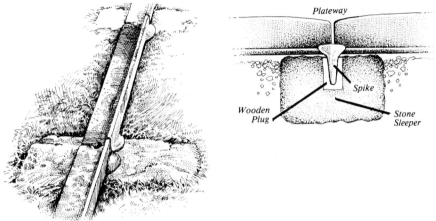

This illustration by Mike Blackmore shows how the tram rails (plateways) were spiked to the stone sleepers.

The very early tram roads used L shaped rails which were designed to guide smooth and non flanged wheels (which were later developed for use on edge rails).

Sleepers were initially cast iron but it was found that these were brittle and liable to snap. Then wood was tried for a while without a lot of success and so in due course rails were mounted on stone blocks using iron saddles or chairs which were fastened to the stone blocks with spikes driven into oak plugs inserted in the block holes.

The cast iron edge rails were 4' long 3" deep 2½" wide and chamfered to 2" wide on the top running surface.

Drivers had to ensure that loads on the trams did not stick out and if an accident occurred and the waggons were derailed the man had to get it back on the track as soon as possible. A jack or lever was generally carried for this purpose.

35

Spragging

"When I grow up I want to be a spragsman like my dad."

"The dangerous art of spragging the trams was one that was handed down from father to son. The network of mountain tram-roads held many inclines since the furnace areas were invariably situated in protected valleys (to obtain improved draught).

The Tumble tram road and the Garnddyrys to the Blorenge bowl tram roads were of a mere one in twenty gradient, just sufficient to assist the horse on the full, downward journey without inconvenience on the return, empty journey. But some inclines by geographical necessity were quite steep.

The spraggers came into being as men who could take the responsibility of shackling the horse behind the tram, leaving it to gallop free while they controlled the downward descent of the load. The sprag was a hardwood beam lying just behind the rear wheels and a few inches above the track. It was linked to a levering bar. By levering on the sprag and locking the rear wheels when required, a good spragger could achieve speeds of up to fifteen miles an hour with a load of five tons of limestone aboard rising to a height of six to eight feet. The masters closed their eyes to speed, but they officially laid the limit of four miles an hour. Speed meant turn-around and higher output, but if a man lost his load he was liable to instant discharge, since it usually meant a blocked line for the time it took to reload it. The spragsmen, once confirmed in their trade, appear to have lost surname identity, being called Jim Spragger Govilon (because he worked the Govilon Incline) or Dafydd Spragger Tumble etc.."

Alexander Cordell
Pages from the Past 1957.

On the left you pass the remains of a small building and then a well constructed retaining wall. It was near this point that the final incline linked up with the tramroad. On this section of tramroad the lines of holed stones are well preserved.

Beyond the Sugar Loaf can be seen the Black Mountains summits of Pen Cerrig Calch and Pen y Gader Fawr. As you progress along the tramroad the view extends even further up through the Vale of Usk towards Mynydd Llangattock, Allt yr Esgair, Mynydd Llangorse and in clear weather the summit of Pen-y-Fan in the Brecon Beacons will show itself in the far distance.

Go through a shallow cutting which leads to a tunnel (which the adventurous may pass through with care, bending heads on entry). The track along the top soon dips down to the other end of the tunnel and the tramroad continues besides a leaning stone wall and contours around the hillside overlooking Cwm Llanwenarth to meet the B 4246. Near here used to stand the Queen Victoria Inn which was frequented by the folk from Garnddyrys.

A local farmer once told me a story of a man who bought this inn just before the second world war and went to the expense of installing electric light. He had a lively party there one night to celebrate the new improvements and whilst someone was thumping a rowdy song out on the piano the floor gave way and everyone including the piano fell into the cellar!

Owing to a fence across the tramroad further on it is now necessary to follow the grass verge of the road up to the second pylon. Then take a track passing through the remnants of a stone wall and then on beside a fence to reach the site of Garnddyrys Forge where you can rejoin Hill's Tramroad.

NOTE
Walkers who have chosen to start from the parking spot on the B 4246 SO 259122 in order to miss out the steep ascents of the Llanfoist inclines should pick up the walk at this point.

Hill's Tramroad in Cwm Ifor showing the old Blacksmith's Shop which at one time was also known as the Tumble Beerhouse.

Follow the tramroad around to the head of Cwm Ifor and cross the stream where the track makes a very tight bend to continue around on the other side of the narrow valley, past weather eroded rocks forming intricate patterns and shapes. Shortly turn sharply left to ascend a rocky path through the rocks above. Looking down you can see the dressed stone supporting wall of the tramroad and ponder on the considerable amount of labour involved in the construction of this transport route.

The track climbs up to reach a stony cart track. Turn left at a corner and head straight up towards the wooden pylons. Now follow a grass verge on the side of the B 4246 to reach Pen-fford-goch pond on the left. This pond was constructed in 1828 and was originally known as "The Forge Pond". It is about 2 acres in size and was built as a header pond to increase the water supply to Garnddyrys Forge. Later, it became known as the "Keeper's Pond" after the Keeper's Cottage that used to stand nearby. This little stone cottage was demolished in about 1970. The keeper's job was to manage the Blorenge grouse moors which are the most southerly in Britain.

Pen-fford-goch Pond, locally known as the "Keeper's Pond".   Chris Barber 1985

It was the Blaenafon Ironworks company who built this spectacular road descending the western side of the Blorenge in 1825. Before then the usual route from Abergavenny to Blaenafon was from Llanellen via the Lower and Upper Ninfa farms. The new road was opened as a Turnpike route and gates were set up for the collection of tolls at Llanfoist, Garnddyrys and Cae White.

Pen-fford-goch means 'the head of the red road' and it would seem that when it was constructed, Old Red Sandstone, which occurs in this vicinity was utilised. The red colour of the road was later even more apparent when red bunker ash from the Garnddyrys furnaces was used for repair work.

38

A tale may be told of an occasion when the hearth stones for some new furnaces at Blaenafon were being brought to the works by road from Staffordshire. But the last of the stones was very late in arriving. It weighed many tons and was being brought at a slow pace up the new road. The haulage contractor was met by a messenger from the Blaenafon works at the sharp bend known as Fiddler's Elbow. He had come to say that there was no need to come any further for suitable stones for the hearth had now been found at Blaenafon. In disgust the haulage man tipped the huge stone off his waggon and it lay on the side of the road until 1847, when it was broken up and used for road building purposes.

Follow a track on the eastern side of the pond and make use of interconnecting sheep tracks to head across country in the general direction of the two radio masts. On reaching a road turn left and follow it to the Foxhunter Car Park (Near the two radio masts).

From the car park a tarmac path leads to a memorial plaque which gives details of the many achievements of Foxhunter — a famous show jumping horse whose skin was buried here by its owner Colonel Harry Llewellyn. Also to be found near this spot is a memorial seat to the Gwent historian Fred J. Hando (1880 - 1970) and a cast iron boundary marker of the Manor of Llanellen.

Follow a well defined footpath in a north easterly direction to reach the summit of the Blorenge which is marked by a trig' point and a large cairn at an altitude of 1,833' (559 metres).

Then continue in a north easterly direction to reach the edge of the escarpment overlooking Llanfoist and Abergavenny.

Follow a wide rutted track to the right which weaves in and out of a series of hollows and humps (old quarry workings) and enjoy a new aspect towards Coed y Prior woods. Further on the track divides. Keep on the wide path and directly ahead on the skyline can be seen a prominent hump which is the Bronze Age burial mound named on the map as Carn y Defaid.

On joining the Llanellen road, turn left to follow the road down with views into the peaceful valley below. After about ½ mile, go left by a cattle grid to cross a stile and follow a bridle path (signposted Llanfoist 3.2km). A wide track is followed for some distance, but just before some trees, where the path descends into a sunken lane, keep left and follow a track down through the field on the left to a gate. Then continue steeply down to meet a stone wall and follow this down, treading a thick carpet of leaves, beneath overhanging trees to suddenly emerge in a very beautiful situation known locally as "The Punchbowl". Before you is a pool reminiscent of a Lakeland tarn set beneath a natural ampitheatre clothed in trees. When the atmospheric conditions are right, a good echo can be obtained here by shouting with gusto at the hillside above. The Punchbowl is the site of a long forgotten quarry, where Old Red Sandstone was once extracted as a source of sand for the local ironworks.

The Punchbowl. Chris Barber 1984

At one time this was also a meeting place for mountain fighters who used to come here to take part in prize fighting contests. They fought with bare fists and wore the scars of previous fights on their flat nosed faces. A look out was always kept posted, for the sport was illegal. The spectators who came here to watch the fun and place bets, used to quietly make their way up the incline from Llanfoist and contour on tracks around the hillside to reach the Punchbowl.

From the lake go up a short rise to a gate and then descend slightly through the next field, past a big heap of stones and on beside a fence. Go past a gate on the right (where a right of way leads down) and then ascend slightly, following the fence to reach another gate. Keep on beside the fence following a wide path to shortly reach another gate. A slight ascent and then the track starts to level out and the views from here are very rewarding.

"The path was lonely and pure with sunlight. Above us reared the mountain with its gorse fanning live in the wind and below us the valley of the Usk lay misted and golden at the foot of Pen-y-Fal."

It is very pleasant walking along this path enjoying an expansive view over Abergavenny and across to the Sugar Loaf and Skirrid Fawr. One may pick out some of the more easily identified buildings in the town such as the castle, Town Hall, Priory Church, Post Office, Nevill Hall Hospital etc. . .

Then on round the north eastern shoulder of the Blorenge and into the great northern bowl of the hill. On reaching the centre of the cwm a stile gives access to the path leading down into Cwm Craf and the incline to Llanfoist. Descend here if you came that way but otherwise continue to your starting point at Garnddyrys. (See page 38 for description of the next part of the route.)

"The hills were April-misted, the old sun red and rosy after his winter sleep. Up to the tram road, down the middle of the Blorenge to Llanfoist Wharf and away down the canal bank where the sheep scamper."

40

WALK 4
BLAENAFON IRONWORKS (3 hours)

Start from Foxhunter Car Park which is situated about half a mile off the B 4246 on the Llanellen road near the two tall radio masts. (SO 264108)

Walk down the road towards Blaenafon for a few yards and then go left to follow a path to the right of the tall masts, heading towards some telegraph poles.

On the skyline to the left can be seen Carn Defaid (literal translation — Carn of the sheep) which is a Bronze Age burial mound where a huge pile of stones probably covers an urn containing the ashes of some long forgotten local chieftain.

The track descends to Blaenavon over an opencast landscape where the ironstone deposits were once removed by 'scouring'. This involved extracting the minerals (which fortunately lay close to the surface) by first removing the turf and then clearing away the top soil by releasing water from above. A lake having been formed by constructing a simple dam above. When the dam was breached the water surged down and scoured the soil away to reveal the iron ore. About 3 tons of ironstone were required to make one ton of iron.

Site of Ironstone scouring above Blaenafon.   *Chris Barber 1984*

"This spot and its vicinity produce abundance of iron, with coal and limestone and every article for smelting the ore; the veins lie in the adjacent rocks, under strata of coal, and are from three and a half to seven or eight inches in thickness; they differ in richness, but yield, upon an average, not less than forty four pounds of pig iron to one hundred weight of ore."

Archdeacon Coxe 1801.

Pig iron is a term used by the early ironworkers, for when the iron from the furnace was cooled in a shape that resembled sleeping pigs and the name became firmly established.

Cast iron is the iron reheated and then moulded into a required shape.

Wrought iron is iron that has been made malleable in order that it may be forged.

Join a stony track which meets the B 4246 just above a cattle grid. Follow a grass verge on the left down towards Blaenafon. Just before some corrugated iron garages go across the road and follow a track over some waste ground. On the left is the Rifleman's Arms (named after military occupation following riots in the town) which may be of interest to you after the walk! When you reach a road go straight across to follow another road downhill.

At a bend by some garages, pause and look down on the remains of the Blaenafon Ironworks. Then follow the road around to the left. Turn right down some steps, past the front of York House and then descend beside the fence of the ironworks to reach a pavement. Go down to the entrance gate, (see page 58 for continuation of route description).

Blaenafon Ironworks 1799. Drawn by Sir Richard Colt Hoare.

The Blaenafon Ironworks (SO 249093) was established in 1789 by Thomas Hill and Thomas Hopkins who leased the land from the Earl of Abergavenny at a rent of £1,300 per year for a 21 year term. It cost £40,000 to build and in 1790 the furnaces started producing pig iron which was initially transported by mule to Newport. Six years later The Monmouthshire Canal was opened between Newport and Pontnewydd. This was linked with the Blaenafon Ironworks by a six mile tram road down the Eastern Valley.

The ironworks has been operating for ten years when this drawing was made. It expanded rapidly during the Napoleonic wars and by 1815 it was the third largest ironworks in South Wales. The biggest were Cyfarthfa and Dowlais at Merthyr Tydfil.

Archdeacon Coxe during his tour of Monmouthshire came here in 1799 and described the scene as follows:—

"At some distance the works have the appearance of a small town surrounded with heaps of ore, coal and limestone and enlivened with all the bustle and activity of an opulent and increasing establishment.

"The view of the buildings which are constructed in the excavations of the rocks is extremely picturesque, and heightened by the volumes of blacksmoke emitted by the furnaces. The coal is so abundant as not only to supply the fuel necessary for the works, but large quantities are sent to Abergavenny, Pontypool and Usk."

"Although these works were only finished in 1789, three hundred and fifty men are employed, and the population of the district exceeds a thousand souls. The hollows of the rocks are strewn with numerous habitations, and the healthy ground converted into fields of corn and pasture."

Thomas Hopkins died in 1789 and his son Samuel, on inheriting a large sum of money decided to build a fine house for himself which he called Ty Mawr (Big House). It was referred to by local people as either The Big House or Blaenafon House. Samuel Hopkins was a popular man in Blaenafon and the town mourned his passing when he died in 1816. His sister Sarah constructed a school in his memory and also taught in it.

In due course, Thomas Hill's son who was also named Thomas, arrived in Blaenafon to help his father run the ironworks. This young man made quite an impression on the town with his extravagant lifestyle but he was also very arrogant and soon became very unpopular. However his life was shortened by drink and rich living and by 1827 both of the Thomas Hills were dead. Then along came the next in line who was yet another Thomas Hill and he took on Robert Wheeley the works manager as his partner. They ran the concern together until 1836 when it was taken over by Robert William Kennard.

By 1840 when the travel writer Nicholson came here on his "Tour of Wales" the works had expanded considerably and he described it as follows:—

"At the works of the Blaenafon Iron Company, five furnaces are all in blast, blown with cold air and six others erecting. This mineral property is one of the best and most valuable in the County of Monmouth, and these works have been distinguished for the superior strength and general excellence of their iron. These five furnaces produce about 400 tons of cast iron per week, and

43

about one half of which is refined, and part of it made into cable iron, and the remainder is sold for tinplates and foundry work. This company is erecting extensive forges and rolling mills". (The last sentence is obviously a reference to the establishment of Garnddyrys Forge.)

Blaenavon Ironworks 1983.

Michael Blackmore's drawing shows the remains of two of the blast furnaces. At one time there were five in operation here. They were built into the hillside so that they could be easily charged from above. Today, these ruins are generally referred to as the finest example of an 18th century ironworks in Europe.

In the early days the blast furnaces were worked with open tops; the waste gases being allowed to escape into the air and at night the whole neighbourhood was illuminated. In later years the gases were collected and utilised for heating the hot air stoves and steam boilers. (one could read a newspaper at night in the street of Blaenafon).

Steam driven blast engines were in use at the beginning of the 19th century and previously water wheels had been used to drive the bellows which provided the blast. It was found that the steam driven engines were much more efficient and this resulted in increased production.

The furnaces were originally fed by hand but at a later date they were mechanically fed by an ingenious system of rip-trams moving on rails along the top edge of the furnaces.

44

1843 was a disastrous year for the Blaenavon company, summed up by the following comment in the Monmouthshire Merlin:—

"The present state of the iron-trade annihilates hope, we see nothing but ruin before us and behind us. The trade must refine within its proper limits, but how that is to be effected — who are to stand, who are to fall — what is to become of the unemployed — how starvation is to be arrested, and the ruin of thousands averted — are questions beyond our provence to unravel, but which must be met boldly in our face because they are not to be avoided — they are already at our door."

Mr. Ashwell, a civil engineer had been appointed to build three new furnaces and blast engines and the stone balance shaft at the end of the furnace yard. However he spent so much money that the capital of the company soon vanished and the works came to a stop. Ashwell then left for pastures new and the owners had to raise fresh capital. The works was then put under the management of Harry Scrivener who during his term of employment wrote a useful book entitled "History of the Iron Trade."

Unfortunately the works still did not prosper and Mr. Scrivener was replaced by Richard Johnson, a brother-in-law of William Crawshay in about 1847. But once again the works came to a stop and fresh capital had to be raised. The management was then placed in the hands of a committee consisting of Thomas Hill, Robert Wheeley and Phillip Jones, a banker who represented the Herberts of Llanarth.

Stack Square, Blaenafon in 1983. Chris Barber.

45

Stack Square.

The two facing rows of four roomed houses were first built in about 1789 to accommodate the skilled workers who had been hired from the Midlands. At a later date the central connecting terrace was constructed and the Company offices were located on the ground floor. On the upper floor, dormitory accommodation was provided for the single workers.

According to the 1851 Census, 84 people lived in the square and no doubt they were all employed by the Blaenafon Ironworks Company. As many as ten people lived in one of these small cottages and one couple actually raised no less than nineteen children here.

This group of houses takes its name from a 60 feet high stack which once stood on the plinth which can be seen in the centre of the square and was connected to a steam engine which supplied the power blast for the furnaces. The stack was demolished in 1912.

Balance Tower and part of Stack square in 1983.   *Chris Barber*

The Balance Tower

This tower operated in a similar manner to the balance shaft at Pwll du quarries. Pipes carried water into a container which by virtue of its own weight lifted a dram loaded with pig iron straight from the casting house to a higher level where it was then transported by rail to Garnddyrys for further attention. The water in the container at the bottom of the tower was then drained away and the weight of the descending dram returned the container back to the top of the tower.

Shepherd Square about 1960 — photograph supplied by Francis Keen.

This was where Alexander Cordell placed the home of the Mortymer family in his novel Rape of the Fair Country. Shepherd Square was situated at the south end of Staffordshire Row and was similar in layout to Stack Square with the houses built on three sides of a court.

The men who worked with horses lived in Stable Yard, Stable Row and Upper Stable Houses. Engine drivers and the mechanics of the new steam age were to be found in Engine Row and Mechanics' Row. These men were very proud of their trades and such identity was very important to them, it even controlled the position in which they sat in chapel.

Bunkers' Row

This used to stand opposite the Rifleman's Arms and consisted of two terraces built end to end in the late 18th century. They were demolished in October 1982.

These cottages stood near the Blaenavon Brickyard that supplied refractory bricks for furnace linings. At one time the employees were largely women who had to work in very grim conditions.

The workers lived in company houses which were built in terraces and sometimes back to back which saved space and time and enabled the builders to make the best use of the sloping ground. River Row was occupied by the colliers. Iron workers resided near their furnaces at Stack Square, Shepherd Square, North Street and Staffordshire Row — which was occupied by specialist workers who had been 'imported' from the Midlands to work at Blaenafon.

Working in very grim conditions these brickyard workers manufactured the refractory bricks which were used for the furnace linings. The Blaenafon brickyard was situated near the Bunker's Row cottages.

Blaenafon Brickworkers in 1880s. Picture supplied by Francis Keen.

Limestone Checkers Cottage, near Blaenafon/Pwll-du tunnel

Tramroad Bridge with arches filled in to provide 'houses' for industrial workers.

When Archdeacon Coxe came here in 1799 his companion Sir Richard Hoare made a drawing which shows a bridge where the five supporting arches had been converted into workers' dwellings. Coxe described the scene as follows:—

"The want of habitations for the increasing number of families, had occasioned an ingenious contrivance: a bridge being drawn across a steep dingle for the support of a railroad leading into a mine, the arches which are ten in number, have been walled up and formed into dwellings."

In contrast he also referred to Ty Mawr. *"I received great marks of hospitality and attention from Mr. Hopkins, one of the proprietors, who is constructing a comfortable and elegant mansion at the northern extremity of this beautiful vale."*

Housing conditions in the Welsh Valleys

"The interior of the houses on the whole clean, food, clothing, furniture — those wants, the supply of which depends on the exertions of each individual, are tolerably well supplied. It is those comforts which only a governing body can bestow are here totally absent. The footways are seldom flagged, the streets are ill-paved and with bad materials and are not lighted. The drainage is very imperfect; there are few underground sewers, no house drains, and the open gutters are not regularly cleaned out. Dust bins and similar receptacles for filth are unknown, the refuse is thrown out in the streets."

Monmouthshire Merlin 1831.

The terraced houses were erected hurriedly on hillsides without drainage systems or decent water supplies. Mountain streams became polluted and piles of household waste and rubbish were dumped indiscriminately, adding to the health problems of the communities, causing outbreaks of fever and cholera.

APPROXIMATE PRICES IN THE COMPANY SHOP IN 1830

2 lbs of mutton	1/-
2 lbs of beef	11d
1 lb of sugar	9d
1 lb of cheese	9d
2 lbs of bacon	1/6

There were Company Shops (known by the workers as 'Tommy Shops') at Garnddyrys, Blaenafon and Pwll-du. The Monmouthshire Merlin on 18th February 1853 reported that they had ceased trading. Later the Garnddyrys and Pwll-du shops were leased by John Harris and Co. in 1861 but went bankrupt in 1863.

The Blaenafon company shop in North Street near the Drum and Monkey was owned and run by the Ironworks Company. This was the only shop in town and all the workers had to spend their hard earned cash there. In 1861 it was leased for the sum of £100 per annum.

"Anything from a pin to a shroud could be bought at such shops and the masters instituted laws by which the workers were forced to buy there, often at prices thirty per cent higher than that of goods offered by private enterprise, which was naturally discouraged if not banned. It is said that a 'Tommy Shop' (as the workers dubbed them) existed at Garnddyrys as early as 1817 near the Garnddyrys Inn.

At these shops the men often purchased with locally minted coin — at Nantyglo, for instance, Crawshay Bailey charged his workers five per cent of their earnings for the privilege of payment in silver. Sometimes they received payment 'in kind' — the bare essentials of life — food and clothing. Thus the early ironworkers found themselves tied body and soul to masters who offered them the alternative of acceptance of the Truck system or starvation."

Alexander Cordell
Pages from the Past 1957.

THE RISING COST OF FOOD (Nothing is new!)
"A public meeting near the 'Big Stone' at Blaenafon considered the high price of butchers' meat and at length passed unanimously a resolution — that no more fresh meat shall be purchased by the working men of Blaenafon until it can be produced at sixpence per pound."

Pontypool and Herald of the Hills Free Press in 1861.

Shopping was all done on credit which in due course was subtracted from the workers' weekly wages which were soon swallowed up and massive debts accumulated creating bitterness and anger.

In 1830 the wages of the employees in Blaenafon were as follows:—

Colliers £1.2.6d per week.
Skilled Ironworkers £2.15s — £3 per week.
7-9 year old boys earned about 4/6 per week.
9-16 year old boys earned about 10/- per week.
Whilst women were only rated 7/6 per week.

Anti-truck laws later abolished the company shops which were undoubtedly the cause of much unrest and ill feeling.

Population of Blaenafon

The population of this town in 1800 was about 1000 and at that time a third of that number worked at the Blaenafon Ironworks. In 1841 the population was 5,115 people. Of these 3,134 were Welsh speaking (61%) and 86 of the people were Irish (1%). 21 people were unable to speak any English at all. By the early 1920's the population rose to 12,500.

"The workmen of all descriptions at these immense ironworks are Welshmen. Their language is almost entirely Welsh. The number of Englishmen among them is very inconsiderable. But the ill effects which large collections of the lower classes produce upon the state of manners, are here very observable, though by no means to so great an extent, as in the manufacturing towns of England.

"The men employed at these works are too much addicted to drinking; but in other respects no great immoralities are to be found amongst them."

H.B. Malkin 1804.

Blaenafon Pubs.

At one time people used to boast that Blaenafon had so many pubs that you could drink in a different one every week of the year! This figure has now been reduced to one pub for every month of the year.

The furnace men consumed very large quantities of liquid — particularly ale, for their work was extremely hot and needed much thirst quenching. They were proud of their trade and were highly respected workers.

The Drum and Monkey Inn mentioned in Cordell's novel (not to be confused with the present day pub of that name on the Black Rock road in the Clydach Gorge) was in North Street. Not far away was the local "clink" or "lock up," run by Mr. Order, Special Constable, which was convenient for drunks who needed calming down for fighting in pubs frequently took place, particularly on pay day when the men were well oiled! Other inns in this vicinity were the New Inn and the Bridgend.

The Lost Pubs of Blaenafon

Albert Inn, Alma, Belle Vue, Boot, Brittania, Brewery Vaults, Bridgend, Crown Inn, Drum and Monkey, Forge Hammer, Forresters, Globe, Greyhound, Griffin, Ivor Castle, Jolly Colliers, King's Arms, King's Head, Lamb Inn, Miner's Arms, Mount Pleasant, Nag's Head, New Inn, New King's Arms, Old Duke, Old Lion Vaults, Old Railway, Oxford, Pen Cefyl, Prince of Wales, Railway, Rising Sun, Rock and Fountain, Royal Arms, Royal Exchange, Royal George, Royal Oak, Star, Swan, Three Cranes, Vine Tree, White Hart, White Horse, White Lion and Winning Horse.

The 'Lock Up'.

Photograph supplied by Francis Keen.

Situated at the north end of Staffordshire Row and built in 1838 this building was a mere 50 yards from the notorious 'Drum and Monkey' inn. The first policeman of Blaenafon to be responsible for this 'lock up' was Mr. Hodder whose name became corrupted very appropriately to Mr. Order.

St. Peter's Church, Blaenafon.   *Chris Barber 1984*

This church was built in 1804 and it is famous for the amount of cast iron used in its construction. It was consecrated on St. Peter's Day in 1805. Before this church was built, the Welsh of Blaenafon mainly worshipped at Capel Newydd which used to stand on the Llanover road and was a very ancient chapel. Its site is marked with an iron cross.

Of special interest inside St. Peter's Church is a memorial to Dr. Samuel Steel who was once the Blaenafon Company doctor until he had an unfortunate accident.

'Sacred to the memory of Dr. Samuel Steel, surgeon of Blaenafon ironworks, who was accidentally killed by a fall from his horse, whilst discharging his professional duties on the 29th day of July 1867 in his 34th year.'

The Steele family for many years provided doctors for the Blaenafon works and they were originally in practice at Tudor Street in Abergavenny. They visited Blaenafon from 1806 several times a week. There is a plaque in memory of them in St. Peter's Church at Blaenafon.

"A medical man from Abergavenny was appointed as surgeon to the works and he and his partner attended there twice a week. On one occasion the surgeon, Dr. Steele, was called to deal with a man whose arm had been cut off. The man had been sitting on the seat in front of the starting handles of a blast engine. He had fallen asleep, presumably as a result of a drinking bout the previous night. The air pump rod passed through the iron floor plates and a projects cotter also passed through a slot just large enough to take it. The man fell off the bench on the upstroke of the engine with his arm across the slot and the descent of the cotter cut it off just above the wrist. He awoke with a start and as he leaned forward the descending cotter cut off another piece of his arm.

The surgeon had to amputate the limb in a third place and the unfortunate man, who was by now quite sober, was told to go home to bed. But apparently he pulled a face and said, "Oh Dr. Steele let me sit up and have a pipe first."

Accidents were frequent in these times when labour was cheap and safety regulations non-existent. Sometimes a man might be splashed by molten iron or a furnace might split under blast, killing or horribly maiming those who were near. Cordell describes such a scene when a man is caught in a furnace explosion at the Nantyglo Ironworks and dies beneath a pile of hot bricks and molten iron.

"Smoke was exploding in mushrooms from the wrecked puddling house, weaving around the shattered roof and condensing in shafts of steam.

Splintered timbers projected from the ruins where the roof slanted drunkenly, and beneath the roof a man was screaming, his voice as shrill as a child's, in short staccato cries, catching his breath to the torture of the scalding . . .A man's face I saw then, in profile at my feet, burned black; a face of marble, drawn clean against the sooted walls of the house, and I knelt, touching it. The flesh of the cheekbone was hot on one side. The other side was melted into streams and the tips of my fingers touched jaw and teeth. Dead, this man, by iron scalding, but the ladle was still in his hand, gripped like a shepherd's crook. Dead, with his legs and hip in the puddling couldron, rigid to the waist where the forty gallons had caught him in its arms of molten iron, and cooling, gripped him."

Furnace men and puddlers frequently went blind at an early age. These strong powerful men, maimed by burns and iron splashes were generally physical wrecks by the age of 40.

EXTRACTS FROM A REPORT OF THE CHILDRENS' EMPLOYMENT COMMISSION OF 1842.

"Mary Davies, near 7 year old, a very pretty girl, was fast asleep under a piece of rock near the air-door below ground. Her lamp had gone out for want of oil. Upon awakening her, she said the rats, or someone, had run away with her bread and cheese, so she went to sleep."

"The boys called Carters are employed in narrow seams of coal in parts of Monmouthshire. Their occupation is to drag the carts or skips of coal from the working place to the main road. In this mode of labour the leather girdle passes round the body and the chain is between the legs, attached to the cart, and the lads drag on all fours."

"Proprietors, agents, foremen, and managers say the regular hours are from eight to ten a day, but some of the overmen say work is seldom finished under eleven to twelve hours. Children and young persons universally declare they never work less than twelve, and occasionally as long as thirteen, fourteen, fifteen, sixteen and even eighteen hours."

"I been down 3 years, when I first went down I could not keep my eyes open. I don't fall asleep now. I smokes my pipe. I smokes half a quarter a week."

William Richards aged 7½ years.

Blaenafon Ironworks in 1895. Picture supplied by Francis Keen

"I have about 37 children working about the furnaces under my charge; the youngest are about 7 years of age. I think I only have one so young as 7 years; he clears the tramroad and is paid by the company five shillings per week. I have some boys from eight to twelve years old helping the 'fillers' at the furnace top, they fill the limestone barrow and assist the filler in pushing it from the yard to the furnace; they do not go into any heat or danger. There are 14 girls from ten to sixteen years of age on the coal and coke yard, they are paid by the Cokers from six shillings to nine shillings per week. There are six boys in the cast-house and refinery from ten to fourteen years. The refinery boys work in some heat in the summer time and sometimes get burned, but not very bad. There are few girls at the mines working below. They all work twelve hours and the furnaces and refineries work all night. There are only four boys and two girls working at night, they change every other week and they all take an hour for dinner and half an hour for breakfast."

William Lloyd the Furnace Manager at Blaenavon.

Forgeside Iron and Steel Works in about 1905.   Picture supplied by Francis Keen.

The new works at Forgeside was commenced in 1858 and opened in 1860. It had many advantages over the old Blaenafon Ironworks. Access was easier and there was more space for development on a fairly level site.

The Garnddyrys forge had proved very inconvenient being so far from the Blaenafon Headquarters and also the distance from Garnddyrys to Newport via the difficult and dangerous inclines was 26 miles. By comparison the distance from Blaenafon to Newport by the new railway down the Eastern Valley was only 16 miles.

Six blast furnaces were constructed on the Forgeside site and a tyre mill was also set up to produce wheels for railway rolling stock. The new works was constructed on freehold land and consequently there was no longer any requirement for the Company to pay ground rent to Lord Abergavenny.

By 1880 the Blaenafon Ironworks had been developed to such a standard that it was regarded as the most modern ironworks in the world. In that year Blaenafon was described as *"a place with an extensive ironworks, abundant collieries, seven blast furnaces and three rolling mills for heavy and light rails, four brick factories, and the adoption of the electric light."*

It used to be said that the world was girdled with Blaenafon iron and this was a reference to the great days of the railway age when Blaenafon was world famous for its superior quality iron rails which were in tremendous demand.

Three other British foundries even had an arrangement with the Blaenafon Company that allowed them to stamp the impressive words "Blaenavon Iron Co." on their rails which was a certain way of ensuring a good sales record. But by 1870 Blaenafon, which had ceased to produce iron rails for the works was not able to compete with the high quality Bessemer steel rails which at this time were being produced at Ebbw Vale.

Blaenafon Ironworks picture supplied by Francis Keen.

The above picture shows the removal of the Blast Furnace facing stones to be used in the construction of St. James Church at Blaenafon. This unfortunate act of vandalism took place in 1911.

In the late 1960s the National Coal Board sold the ironworks site to Blaenafon Urban District Council for land reclamation. Stack Square was declared unfit for habitation and the residents were rehoused. In 1972 the Department of the Environment took the site into their care and work started in 1974 on consolidating the remaining buildings with the intention of turning the site into a museum.

Outside the ironworks, follow the pavement and take the next turning on the right. (Notice on the right the "Ironworks Remains Car Park" which provides an alternative starting point for this walk or to be used if you just wish to visit the Blaenafon Ironworks).

Continue along the pavement to reach the Brynmawr road. Turn left and shortly cross the road to follow a tarmac lane up to two houses. Just in front of the first house go up to a stile and on the other side ascend a short incline.

Remains of Incline Braking System on tramroad to Hill Pits.   Photograph Chris Barber — 1983.

At the top of the incline on the right can be seem the remains of the braking system which controlled the rate of descent of the trams. Only a small part of this device remains to be seen, but it was obviously an ingenious system, well engineered and constructed of wrought and cast-iron. It was excavated in 1979 by John Van Laun during a Department of Extra Mural Studies course sponsored by University Cardiff.

Just to the north of the brake can be seen the remains of a small building which no doubt provided shelter for the brake man who operated a lever linked to the brake wheel.

The path soon links in with another track which shortly levels out providing good views across to Coity Mountain and Big Pit. Across to the left can be seen the remnants of the village of Garn-yr-Erw.

The area of land above Garn-yr-Erw is known as "The Patches". Here can be seen the surface workings where men once dug for ironstone which was found embedded in the shale. When these sources of ironstone became unprofitable to work, by the middle of the 19th century, the Blaenafon furnaces were fed with imported ores from Spain. It was found that the Spanish ores were more suitable than the Welsh material when used in the Bessemer furnaces which were introduced after 1860.

Walk on towards a stone stack which is perfectly square and constructed of large blocks of dressed stone. 'There is a tree growing out of the top.

59

This is the site of Hill Pits which were sunk in the late 1830s to produce ironstone and coal for the Blaenafon Ironworks. It took its name from the hillside location (situated at an altitude of 1,420 feet above sea level) rather than the actual Hill family. (SO 239102).

The twin shafts were filled in about twenty years ago and the stone stack which is well constructed of dressed stone (about 6 feet square and 20 feet high) was once linked with a boiler house.

Previously there had been a certain amount of mining undertaken in this vicinity and there was a coal level worked near the smallholding of Tyr Abraham Harry, which is the obvious ruin on the hillside above.

A tram road led from Hill Pits to an incline of approximately 1 in 6 (which you have just ascended) and a tram road led on from there to the Blaenafon Ironworks.

To the north east of the tramroad is a small pond which was the water supply used for steam power at the Pits.

"God made the world, but the devil made coal and hid it in the innermost recesses of the earth, that he might drive man mad with searching for it.

Old Welsh collier.

The ironmasters were the first pioneers of the Welsh coal trade for when it became difficult to obtain wood for fuel the iron trade declined until it was discovered that coke was an even better fuel than wood for smelting purposes. This resulted in a great revival in the coal trade.

Consequently the ironmasters did much to develop the mining of coal and sank many mines to supply themselves with coal (in the form of coke) for their great ironworks. The surplus coal was sold to other ironworks and in due course coal took over as an even more important and prosperous industry than iron making.

In its heyday Blaenafon was producing half a million tons of coal a year and its high quality steam coal was used in steam engines and steam ships, all over the world.

Continue along the track to pass a pool with a small concrete dam. Ahead now is a present day opencast mining operation. Just past the pool turn right to follow a well defined tramroad incline which heads straight up to the skyline. The start may be wet and muddy in places due to a stream.

This incline is half a mile long and it once consisted of four lines of rails laid with a 4′ 8½″ gauge. An engine with four wire ropes to haul the trams was mounted on the top of the ridge. The system worked as follows:—

One truck was ready loaded at the bottom. Two trucks were on the summit (one full and one empty) and the truck at the Pwll-du side of the ridge was empty. In this position, and at the sound of a bell signal the engine would be set in motion and all four trucks would start moving at the same time. They were loaded at the Garn yr Erw side and unloaded at Pwll-du.

On one occasion an operator was careless and a truck was allowed to slip over the top without a rope attached on the Garn-yr-Erw side. It hurtled down the incline and amazingly stayed on the rails all the way, in spite of efforts made by some plate layers to make it jump off the rails by throwing sleepers on the line. At the bottom of the incline, the runaway truck cut through an embankment about 30′ wide and 4′6″ deep and half buried itself. These trucks were so sturdily built that after being dug out and a new axle and a set of wheels fitted it was back on the incline again the following day.

Ascend the incline and on the skyline you will pass through a cutting to reach the crest of the ridge. Here you may enjoy extensive views across to the Brecon Beacons, the Black Mountains and the summit of the Blorenge.

The landscape here is scarred by opencast mining but the hollows in the ground have now grassed over. At a junction of tracks, go straight on and then down past a brick building. Unfortunately, sections of the old incline have been dug away on this side of the hill, but tracks lead down towards a white building directly below which is the old Lamb Inn of Pwll-du.

On reaching the road, turn right and walk back to the starting point via Pen-fford-goch Pond (Keeper's Pond).

"The Autumn nights were drawing in and dusk and bats were dropping around us. Behind was the red glow, before us the hills shone and sparkled, with men working like demons against the glare, and as we came nearer town the night-shift going up the Turnpike was whispering in the wind." A.C.

WALK 5
Crawshay Bailey's Towers (1½ hours)

To reach the starting point of this walk from Brynmawr; drive south along the A 467 to reach Nantyglo. Turn right by the Wesleyan Chapel to reach Roundhouse Close. Take the second turning on the left and then shortly bear right along a gravel track. Soon you will see a round stone tower directly ahead. There is a small space for parking on the side of the track just before the tower.

Walk along the track to the left of the tower and shortly branch left to pass some houses. Ahead will be seen a metal gate. Here you can stand and look across at the site of Nantyglo House.

Nantyglo House in about 1900.   *Picture supplied by Trevor Rowson*

The Nantyglo Ironworks which was situated in the valley below, was opened in 1795 and subsequently purchased by Joseph Bailey in 1811. His brother Crawshay joined him as a partner in 1813. Under their joint ownership the works quickly developed into one of the largest and most efficient in the world. The Bailey brothers soon amassed a fortune.

Nantyglo House (otherwise known as Ty Mawr or Crawshay House) was a fine mansion built by the Bailey brothers. They chose an elevated but sheltered site near the small house built by Mr. Harford who was the first ironmaster of the Nantyglo works. They later turned his former home into servants' quarters.

Their new mansion had a fine colonnaded front supported by six iron pillars cast in their own works and inside was a magnificent marble staircase. The grounds were carefully landscaped and the driveway passed through an impressive avenue of trees.

Crawshay Bailey's Round Tower at Nantyglo.

They must have felt uneasy in their great mansion after the Merthyr uprising in 1813 and in order to protect themselves and their families from their own workers in times of trouble, they constructed in 1816, two fortified towers. To provide immediate access it is claimed that they even linked their fine mansion with one of the towers by constructing an underground passage. However this tunnel has yet to be discovered.

The stables of the mansion can still be seen and also the remnants of the two towers but the house itself was demolished during the second world war and the stone was taken away for other building purposes. Excavations on the site of the mansion have been carried out in recent years by Nantyglo Senior Comprehensive School.

In 1830 Joseph Bailey retired from the management of the works and moved to Glan Usk Estate near Crickhowell. Crawshay Bailey continued to live at his Nantyglo mansion until 1860 when he retired to Llanfoist House.

Nantyglo House was then occupied by the managers of the Nantyglo and Blaina Iron and Coal Company until 1885. After that date it ceased to be lived in, and gradually became a ruin. During the Second World War it was demolished and the stone used for building purposes and road construction.

Go right beside a stone wall and follow a path which leads up to a wide track where you turn left. Above now can be seen the other round tower which is unfortunately in imminent danger of collapse. Continue along the track looking down on the site of Nantyglo House. On the right is a small stone building which used to be the gardener's cottage. Walk on to reach a gate and follow a cart track. The valley below was once dominated by the massive Nantyglo Ironworks belching smoke and flames to the sky.

Nantyglo Ironworks in 1820.

"This was the Bailey empire where the iron bubbles into a thousand moulds. Sweat pours here, beer is taken by the gallon, men die in mutilation, children are old at ten. Eyes are put out here, sleeves are tied with string. The turrets of the ironmaster's house were stark black against the glow, the windows glinting, his defence towers threatening any challenge. From Cwm Crachen to Coalbrookvale was a river of fire. Ash drifted past the window, settling like snow." A.C.

In 1869 Clarke came here and in his "History of Monmouthshire" he gave the following description of the Nantyglo Ironworks:—

"The great seat of the iron district. Nearly the whole of the population is employed in the extensive works of Messrs Joseph and Crawshay Bailey, which comprises seven blast furnaces, four rolling mills, and nearly one hundred puddling furnaces — where iron of every description is manufactured."

The following year John Murray came to Nantyglo and in his "Handbook to South Wales" he observed:—

"Here are the large ironworks of Messrs J. & C. Bailey from which immense fortunes have been made by that family. But they present a sad contrast with some of the other great establishments, being exceedingly dirty, slovenly and dilapidated."

When Crawshay Bailey died in 1872 the Nantyglo works became the Nantyglo and Blaina Iron and Coal Company.

In 1872 the Nantyglo works was sold to the Nantyglo and Blaina Ironworks Company for £300,000, but it eventually closed in 1878 and was entirely dismantled with all machinery and even scraps of iron being sold off to meet the demands of the creditors. Only the empty buildings were left.

Go through a metal gate and follow the fence on your right up to a stile. The ruined house in the trees over to the left is Coalbrookvale once the home of George Brewer another ironmaster.

From the stile go straight up to pass a small gate in the fence, which is followed to the right. This is a good vantage point. Below can be seen the two round towers and the large stable block where the Baileys kept their horses and carriages. To the north can be seen the sprawling town of Brynmawr, which incidently is the highest town in Wales, where winter comes early and is very prolonged. Beyond Brynmawr is the mass of Mynydd Llangynidr which is honeycombed with caves and contains the twenty mile system of Agen Allwedd, which is one of the longest caves in Britain.

Strike across to a stile in the fence on the left and then follow a path on the edge of the Nantyglo Golf Course. This is claimed to be the highest golf course in England and Wales where the 14th hole is at an altitude of about 1500′ and is known as the "Crow's Nest"!

Follow a path down to join a gravel track which descends past numerous shacks where chickens wander freely. This is not a very tidy landscape but it provides a fascinating insight into the life of the Nantyglo hill folk. On reaching a tarmac road, turn right to walk back to your starting point.

"There is no green on the mountain after dark. Sulphur is in the wind then, and the sky is red with furnace glare all over the ridges from Nantyglo to Risca and when the nightshift comes on the world catches alight." A.C.

WALK 6
The Chartists' Cave (3 hours)

Leave your car at a car park on the B 4560 (SO 156172). Walk up the road towards Beaufort to reach a gravel track on the right (SO 161164). This leads to a small abandoned quarry with a smooth rock floor. A cave entrance resembling the mouth of a railway tunnel can be seen in the rock face of the quarry. This is Blaen Onneu cave which extends for about one hundred and fifty feet and may be examined with care. On the right hand side of the quarry floor is a pothole — generally covered by a boulder — to prevent sheep or careless walkers dropping inside.

Scramble up a sheep track to the left of the cave to the open moor above. Now walk in a south westerly direction until a prominent cairn is sighted. On reaching this point; the trig' point (SO 148159) at spot height 1,773′ should be visible. Otherwise a compass bearing is essential if visibility is poor. From the trig' point follow a path towards Garn Fawr which appears as a hump on the ridge two miles away. (In poor visibility walk on a compass bearing directly to the Chartist' Cave). The path soon disappears and numerous swallet holes are passed on this route, these circular depressions are caused by the roofs of underground chambers collapsing.

The Mouth of the Chartists' Cave.   *Chris Barber 1977*

On reaching Garn Fawr, 1,805′, walk north-east to reach a low cliff where the Chartists' cave may be found. The entrance is about six feet high, below a rock

66

arch (SO 127153). Inside is a chamber providing excellent shelter and two passages leading to chambers deeper in the cave. It is reputed to have been used by the Chartists as a meeting place and ammunition store prior to their historic march on Newport in 1839.

Picture now, Iestyn Mortymer riding on a Chartist horse with Abraham Thomas over the hills from Blaenavon to reach the moors of Mynydd Llangynidr . . .

"It was midnight when we struck the tramroad near Llangattock, and the trams were rumbling under a misty moon, limestone on top, muskets underneath, and one in every six carrying powder and shot. Down the line of trams we went to the cave entrance where a man was standing guard. Big and broad he was in the shadows with the smoke of his clay curling up in the still air.

I tethered my horse and followed him in. It was a cavern inside, a fissure cut through solid limestone by the rushing waters of a world melting from ice a hundred million years ago; a weird place of grotesque shadows and chilling echoes where the only light was flung by lanterns. Deeper into the mountain we went, through cavern after cavern where men sat at tables pouching shot and filling powder-horns. Deeper still, crouching at times, we reached the gunsmiths' rooms where skilled men fitted barrels to stocks of pistols and muskets. On into the bowels of Mynydd Llangynidr, and into the pit of hell itself. Here were the blacksmiths, stripped and sweating, and the air was ringing to the beat of hammers. Here red iron was hammered into steel. Here in neat rows, were the pike-heads and spears that were to wrest power from the aristocracy and give it to the people. I saw men armed, coming and going with missions of importance. And on the tramroad outside the arms were being loaded and transported to all the valleys of Gwent." A.C.

One may either return by the same route or by the following alternative to give variety to the walk. Head in a north-easterly direction to reach the rim of Blaen Cwm-claisfer. Contour around the heather-covered and rocky slopes to reach the base of a limestone escarpment, then follow a track alongside a stone wall above the forestry plantation to reach an old tram road leading past the Blaen Onneu quarries. On reaching a tarmac road your starting point is not far away.

N.B.: It should be emphasised that care should be taken on these moors in misty weather and without the help of a compass (and the ability to use it) walkers may lose their sense of direction and exhaust themselves walking in circles.

Background to the Chartists' Uprising.

Throughout the country thousands of men supported the Chartists' cause for they believed that this was the way to obtain higher wages, better food and living conditions. Their petition drawn up in 1837 and known as "The Peoples' Charter" contained six demands:—

1. That every man of full age should have a vote.
2. That the property qualification for entry to Parliament should be abolished, which would enable even a poor man to be eligible for election.
3. That Members of Parliament should be paid.
4. That voting should be by secret ballot.
5. That there should be equal electoral districts.
6. That Parliament should be re-elected every year.

They succeeded in obtaining more than a million signatures to their petition. However, when it was presented to Parliament the members refused to give it consideration. Subsequently riots broke out throughout the country and the disappointed people decided that the only way to achieve their demands would be through force and bloodshed.

The Chartists of Gwent held meetings at Newport, Pontypool Blackwood, Monmouth and many other places. Eloquent speakers explained the principles of the Charter and urged communities to arm themselves to obtain their demands by force.

A plan of attack was drawn up at a secret meeting held at the Coach and Horses in Blackwood. It was decided that all supporters of the Charter should arm themselves and assemble on the night of Sunday November 3rd 1839 and march on Newport in three divisions. John Frost was to lead the Blackwood section. The men from Blaenafon, Abersychan and that general area were to march under the command of William Jones. The third division would be made up of men from Brynmawr, Ebbw Vale and district and would be led by Zephanaiah Williams who kept a beer-house at Coalbrookvale, Nantyglo.

The three divisions would rendezvous at the Cefn (about two miles from Newport) and then march upon the sleeping town, where it was foolishly believed that the inhabitants would be completely unaware of the impending attack.

First they would overcome the soldiers and obtain possession of the town. Then they would destroy the bridge across the Usk with explosives to prevent the Welsh Mail from reaching Birmingham. When the mail failed to arrive in that Midland town, this would represent a signal to the Chartists there that the Monmouthshire uprising had been successful. They would then attempt a similar campaign which it was hoped would be extended throughout the country.

"The pot that had simmered for fifty years boiled over. Colliers and miners, furnacemen and tram-road labourers were flooding down the valleys to the Chartists' rendezvous; men from Dowlais under the Guests, Cyfarthfa under the Crawshays, Nantyglo under Bailey and a thousand forges and bloomeries in the hills; men of the farming Welsh, the Staffordshire specialists and the labouring Irish were taking to arms." A.C.

Some of the men blackened their faces with soot or wore masks and they were all armed with anything they could lay their hands on which might serve as a weapon, ranging from old muskets to crowbars.

"Every ironworks on The Top from Hirwaun to Blaenafon was on strike, every furnace blown out, and owners who challenged were kicked aside or beaten. In the rain we gathered, lawless leaderless, seeking Zephaniah Williams. We were the men of the valleys three thousand strong it was said." A.C.

People who did not sympathise with the Chartists' cause fled to safety or hid in a wide assortment of hiding places, such as oak chests, disused coal levels — even up trees!

The marching men entered houses to persuade the mature male occupants to join them; using force where necessary and all places of likely concealment were searched.

During the Newport march the Chartists adopted the word "Beanswell" as their password. Any stranger greated with the word "Beans" was expected to reply "Well". If he failed to reply in this way he would be taken prisoner as an enemy of the cause.

Arriving at Newport they marched down Stow Hill to open their initial attack on the Westgate Hotel. But inside was Thomas Philips the Mayor who had occupied the premises with a detachment of twenty eight men of the 45th regiment and a small force of special constables.

Storming the Westgate Hotel in Newport. 19th Century Engraving.

The marchers were to have entered Newport at 2 o'clock in the morning but they did not arrive until 8.30 a.m. Bedraggled and weary they marched into the square in front of the Westgate, armed with muskets, picks, pitchforks and cudgels the mayor stood bravely in the doorway and demanded to know their grievances.

A Chartist opened fire at one of the Special Constables and inspired the mob into action. The Special Constables in the Westgate panicked and hid themselves in different parts of the building. One hid inside a copper boiler and did not emerge until the riot was over. Some escaped from the rear of the building and ran home.

The Chartists opening volley wounded several soldiers and Mayor Phillips received a shot in the hip. The Chartists pounded on the door but their confidence rapidly vanished, when on an order from the mayor the soldiers opened fire. After a few volleys from the windows and down the passage towards the door of the hotel the riot was quickly dispersed.

"Behind us the Chartists were dead or wounded, before us they lay under the scorching fire of the Redcoats. Only one fired back now, a man with one leg, the last broken hero of the Chartist cause." A.C.

The wet and weary men had little heart for a fight after their long march through the pouring rain the previous night, and fled in all directions. They threw weapons on the ground and bolted, leaving their wounded companions groaning, moaning and dying. It was all over in 25 minutes.

"They took us to the stable yard, the first prisoners of the Westgate, and they herded the rest in after us. Hour after hour they were brought in from tram roads as far as Pye Corner; broken, dejected men and boys, soaked and weary, many of them wounded; silent, unprotesting under the musket-butts of the Redcoats. I saw in their grey faces of defeat the tragedy of my generation." A.C.

Twenty two Chartists were killed outside the Westgate Hotel and many were wounded. It is thought that many more dead were taken away by their comrades and secretly buried to protect their families. Scattered around the street outside was a wide assortment of weapons which included:— pistols, blunderbusses, swords, bayonets, pikes, spears, daggers, billhooks, axes, cleavers, pitchforks, scythes, saws, bludgeons, sledgehammers and mandrills.

The survivors scattered and fled to hide in Wentwood and the local hills of Twmbarlwm and Mynydd Maen. Thirty-eight men were subsequently arrested and brought to trial by a special commission at Monmouth. Rumours spread that an attempt would be made to rescue Henry Vincent, one of their leaders and other prisoners from Monmouth Gaol but the Chartists abandoned the plan.

It was not many days before the leaders were captured and brought to trial. Frost, Williams and Jones were sentenced to be hanged drawn and quartered, but their lives were spared, and they were sentenced to transportation for life. (In 1854 they were granted a free pardon).

Mayor Phillips as a reward for his bravery received a knighthood and he was also presented with a silver plate valued at 800 guineas. In addition he was awarded the freedom of the City of London. His grave can be seen in the churchyard at Llanellen, near Abergavenny.

The sudden collapse of the Newport riot helped to bring the Chartist movement to an end but in years to come their grievances were recognised and all but one of the points of their charter (Annual Parliaments) are law today.

The dead men who were identified were:—
William Williams (Cwm Tillery), Abraham Thomas (Coalbrookvale), William Evans (Tredegar), Isaac Thomas (Nantyglo), William Griffiths (Merthyr Tydfil), William Farraday (Blackwood) and George Shell (Pontypool).

They were buried on the north side of St. Mary's Chapel in the churchyard of St. Woolos, Newport. Their graves were decorated on Sunday 12th April 1840 with wreaths and the following verse was displayed:—

> May the rose of England never blow
> The Clyde of Scotland cease to flow
> The harp of Ireland never play
> Until the Chartists gain the day.

Mosaic depicting the Chartists' March. *Chris Barber 1983*

In Newport today the Chartists' riots are remembered by this imaginative mosaic depicting their march on the town. It can be seen on the edge of John Frost Square and nearby is an office block reaching to the sky which has been named the Chartist Tower.

Several relics of the riots can be seen in Newport Museum (entrance in John Frost Square) and the present Westgate Hotel stands on the site of the old Westgate Inn. The wooden pillars of the old porch have been preserved inside for they show bullet holes made by the Chartists' muskets.

"It may be said that the Chartist agitation which had for its object the reform of Parliament — was so much energy wasted. I think not. The Chartist influence extended beyond the six points, and to it we largely owe the extirpation of innumerable, some of the abominable abuses, and a great widening of the bounds of freedom."

George Julian Harney, A Chartist Leader writing in 1897.

The Puddlers' Arms
A small inn situated on the Keeper's Road, just above Fiddler's Elbow. Ironworkers travelling down to Abergavenny and back must have sunk many a quart in here. Unfortunately it was demolished many years ago. This drawing was based on a photograph taken of the ruined inn by Alexander Cordell in 1955.

MISCELLANEOUS INFORMATION

Big Pit Mining Museum
Blaenafon Gwent. (SO 238087)

Photograph 1984 — Chris Barber.

By 1873 the Blaenafon Company were operating sixteen collieries in addition to the ironworks. Coal mining was very profitable at this time for this was the age of steam and coal was needed to power steam engines of many types used for a wide variety of purposes throughout the world.

Big Pit was established in 1880 by making Kearsley's Pit which had been sunk in 1860 much deeper and this became the most important of the pits owned by the Blaenafon company.

The mine was closed in 1980 when the reserves became exhausted and operations at Big Pit came to an end after 100 years of production. A decision was made to turn the site into a mining museum and the restoration and preservation of Big Pit has been carried out by the Big Pit Museum Trust, a non profit-making charitable body. Support to the scheme has been given by:—

The Borough of Torfaen, Gwent County Council, the European Regional Development Fund, National Coal Board, National Heritage Memorial Fund, National Museum of Wales, Council of Museums in Wales, Wales Tourist Board, Welsh Development Agency and the Welsh Office.

Big Pit is unique as an industrial museum. It can be seen as it was on its last working day. Many of the men who previously worked in the mine now act as guides and they help to bring the old mine back to life providing vivid descriptions and amusing anecdotes of their working memories of Big Pit.

Visitors are able to undertake an underground tour of the mine in complete safety, descending in the pit cage down a 300 feet deep shaft. Wearing helmets and cap lamps the tourists are given the opportunity of experiencing the world of one hundred years of coal mining. The underground tour includes coal faces, massive underground engines, stables for the pit ponies and old ironstone workings. It is an experience to remember and you are advised to wear stout shoes and warm clothes.

Forgeside Blaenafon

Brittle steel was caused by phosphorus which was contained in the majority of iron ore but the big question facing these early steel makers was how to remove the phosphorus.

Sidney Gilchrist Thomas was the man who found the solution to this problem. He seemed a most unlikely person to do so for he lived in London and worked as a Justice's Clerk. However his cousin Percy Gilchrist worked at the Blaenafon Works and Sidney, who was an enthusiastic chemist made the journey from London to Blaenafon on a regular basis in his spare time during 1877 to work in the laboratories there with his cousin. His aim was to solve the world wide phosphorus problem. He was successful in his task and found the solution by constructing and developing a new furnace lining of dolomite and tar.

This discovery brought him fame and considerable wealth but unfortunately he died of tuberculosis at the age of 34.

Carnegie the industrial entrepreneur, once said *"These two men, Thomas and Gilchrist of Blaenavon, did more for Britain's greatness than all the kings and queens put together. Moses struck the rock and brought forth water. They struck the useless phosphoric ore and transformed it into steel — a far greater miracle."*

Bessemer converters at Forgeside in 1896.

Blaenafon extinguished its last furnace in 1938. The local reserves of iron had long become depleted and the cost of transporting imported iron ore from the coast to the works high up in the Eastern Valley had become too expensive. The future now lay in the erection of new large steel works in the coastal regions of South Wales.

Postscript Jottings from Alexander Cordell.

Pwll-du Tunnel
It is claimed that the Garnddyrys women would shorten their journey to Blaenavon to do their shopping by making use of the Pwll-du tunnel.

Beware of the "tylwyth teg".
There is a fable of a person who one evening was walking from Abergavenny to Blaenavon past the Balance Pond (where Iestyn fought) and he swore that he saw the tylwyth teg sliding on the frozen pond playing 'touch me at last' — their lips stained black through eating winberries. 'Winberries in December' he exclaimed. 'It's enough to frighten decent folk to death'! He said that the tylwyth teg were as naked as babies, with silver hair and fingernails; all this he readily accepted, but not the winberries.

A cottage for the fairies.
Many of the colliers believed in fairies. Take for example the man who wouldn't go out at night without a mate because fairies had been seen sitting on the chimney pots. The colliers were so worried about the tylwyth teg that they even built a quarter-sized cottage for them, so that they would keep away 'from decent people' and live by themselves.

Jesus walks the Blorenge.
A man named Stinchcombe was injured in an underground accident. Feeling very depressed he went up to the Blorenge to commit suicide. It was Christmas and he and his wife were trying to live on seven shillings a week and were starving. At the top of the hill (near where the radio masts now stand) he later swore that he met a man who left no footprints in the snow, who gave him five shillings and told him that he should be ashamed of himself for his wife's courage. Stinchcombe then went home and found that the Quakers had called and left coal and food. He said that the man was Jesus by face and form and despite the bitter weather he was only wearing a robe.

The Virgin Mary Cave
In a curve on the Nantyglo tramroad there used to be a cave with a strange structure in it like a statue of the Virgin Mary. The colliers used to go inside and pray to it. But because it wasted working time, Crawshay Bailey sent some men to destroy the image.

Cannon Balls and Slaves
Anthony Bacon, an early ironmaster sold cannon balls to the British Army and also to the French. He transported them down the Blorenge incline to Newport and from Dover to the French ports. In his early days he was also a slave owner, as was Lord Penrhyn of Bangor, and like him, received Treasury compensation when slavery was abolished at a rate of so much per slave freed.

A short hard life.
The expectancy of life in Blaenafon and Nantyglo in 1849 was twenty one years. One child in four died before the age of two. In Merthyr at the same time life expectancy was under sixteen years. The main causes of death were cholera and typhoid.

Night time Experiments at Forgeside.
Within the entrance to Forgeside at the top of North Street there used to be a
small red brick building where Sidney Gilchrist Thomas and his cousin
Gilchrist Thomas carried out their experiments. A collier, aged ninety, (in
1956) told me that his father distinctly remembered the Gilchrist cousins
carrying out phosphorus extraction experiments with little iron crucibles in
1877. It was possible to see them working into the dawn from the window of
the Drum and Monkey and the flashing 'lighted up the windows of
Staffordshire Row even when the furnaces were blown for hearth cleaning.'

Surrounded by slag.
Close to Crawshay Bailey's mansion in Nantyglo was a tipping area which
gradually spread from the works to the south. It encroached upon the house of
a man who lived with his family in the very path of the spreading tip. Even
though it threatened his house the man defied Crawshay Bailey to remove him.
So the Agent saw to it that this man's house was surrounded on three sides by a
glowing tip some twenty feet high. The slag was carefully banked so that it
wouldn't slide down and burn him out and in this way more and more heat was
generated until the man was forced to evacuate the house he owned.

People with pride and a sense of humour.
A crippled overman told me that, when he was ten years old (in about 1870) his
mother, when sending him to get groceries from the Company Shop next door
to the Drum and Monkey, used to give him a piece of black cloth to put over
the purchases, 'For it isn't every woman who wants neighbours peeping down
from upstairs windows, counting up the cost of groceries and putting it around
the back rows of Calfaria on a Sunday night.'

Stack Square — a warm spot to live!
There were small underground chambers radiating from the base of the great
chimney which once stood in the centre of Stack Square (see page 46). They
collected the hot fumes before emission at height; thus providing a form of
district central heating system for the cottages built in a U shape around the
base of the stack.

The Gran of Shepherd's Square.
Before Shepherd's Square was demolished, a housewife told me that, at the
junction of the last cottage with North Street there was a deep recess in the
wall, probably a sitting point for a tall man; In this recess, for many years
there lived an old woman dressed in black. This was her home and she greeted
people coming and going, asking nothing of anyone although she accepted
food. One Winter she was found frozen to death; her name was linked with a
ten year old boy who was found dead of starvation on Christmas Day
morning. This was in living memory.

Politics and Riots.
Blaenafon Square, near the Rolling Mill pub, was a site of many of the Union
and political meetings of the industrial years. During a riot in the town, beer
barrels were rolled out of the Rolling Mill and split open. It is said that the
locals were in tears at the sight of the ale pouring down High Street.

The Whistle Inn

Not far from Big Pit Mining Museum is a very old pub called the Whistle Inn. This is an ideal resting place between Blaenafon and Nantyglo, where Iestyn called in for a pint on his way to his marriage to Mari at St. Peter's, Blaenafon.

"Mari Dirion! How lovely was her name. I said it aloud to the rhythm of Elot's hoof-beats on the mountain turf. Spurring her, we made a gallop, entering a line of firs standing bright green and misted in the growing heat, then we swung across the mountain to the Whistle Inn. A pint to settle the dust, a pail of spring water for Elot, and a sleep beneath a tree. . ." A.C.

The present Landlords of The Whistle are most friendly people, who have a son rejoicing in the nickname of 'Dai Tomorrow,' because, his mother says, he will never do today that which can be put off until tomorrow. This public house (no accommodation) has the finest collection of miners' lamps in Wales — they have been seen on television.

DATES OF LOCAL INDUSTRIAL EVENTS

1782 The Blaenafon Coal and Iron Company is formed by Thomas Hill and Samuel Hopkins.

1789 The first furnace in Blaenafon comes into operation. Nantyglo Ironworks opens.

1790-92 Blaenafon Ironworks produces an average of 3,600 tons of iron per year.

1795 Tram road constructed from Blaenafon works to Pontnewynydd.

1796 Output at Blaenafon Ironworks is increased to 4,318 tons per year.

1798 Monmouthshire Canal completed (Newport to Pontypool).

1800 Archdeacon Coxe visits Blaenafon. Population in Blaenafon 1,000.

1802 Monmouthshire Canal extended to Pontnewynydd.

1805 St. Peter's Church in Blaenafon is built by Thomas Hill and Samuel Hopkins.

1811 Nantyglo Ironworks is sub-let to Joseph Bailey, Crawshay Bailey and Matthew Wayne.

1812 Brecon and Abergavenny Canal is joined with Monmouthshire Canal. 14,579 tons of iron were sent by canal to Newport during this year, (compared with 1,090 tons in 1801).

1815 Battle of Waterloo. This was followed by an industrial slump in Britain. Death of Samuel Hopkins.

1816 Welsh Ironmasters make threats to reduce wages. The workers down tools and hold meetings.
A school is built in Blaenafon by Sarah Hopkins in memory of her brother Samuel.

1817 Garnddyrys Forge is completed and production begins.

1824 Death of Thomas Hill the first.

1825 Turnpike road from Blaenafon to Abergavenny constructed. (Now the B 4246).
Nantyglo becomes the leading iron producing works in Gwent.

1827 Garn Derris Iron Company formed.
Death of Thomas Hill the second.

1828 Forge Pond constructed. (Now known as Keeper's Pond).

1829 Anti-Chartist meeting held at Coalbrookvale with Crawshay Bailey in the chair.

1830 Skilled ironworkers at Blaenafon are now earning £2.15s - £3 per week.
9,937 tons of iron from Blaenafon is transported by canal. The figure for the same year from Garnddyrys is 3,654 tons. (Between 1817-1840 the figure for Garnddyrys is 94,808 tons).

1836 R.W. Kennard takes over the Blaenafon Ironworks and forms the Blaenafon Coal and Iron Company Ltd.

1837 The Peoples' Charter is drawn up by the Chartists.

1838 A "lock-up" is built in North Street at Blaenafon.
14 men and 2 women drown in Cinder Pit at Blaenafon.

1839 3/4 November Chartists' uprising and march on Newport.
Mass trial of the Chartists held at Newport.

1842 Mines Act passed by Parliament.

1847 Forgeside, Blaenafon established for smelting operations.

1850 Population of Blaenafon 4,000
The Blaenafon — Pwll-du incline is reconstructed by Thomas Dyne Steel to use standard gauge waggons.

1852 The Great Western Railway Line from Newport to Pontypool is completed.

1853 Decision made to move the forge at Garnddyrys to Forgeside, Blaenafon.

1854 Blaenafon to Pontypool Railway opened.
John Frost the Chartist leader receives an unconditional pardon.

1856 Henry Bessemer invents a new process for making steel.

1857 Crumlin Viaduct is opened. Blaenafon iron was used for this enormous project.

1860 Garnddyrys Forge is dismantled.
Canal bank at Llanfoist collapses.
Population of Blaenafon 7,500.
Big Pit is opened.

1862 Blaenafon Town Hall opened in Lion Street.
New forge in operation at Forgeside.

1867 Dr. Samuel Steel, surgeon of Blaenafon Ironworks dies after falling off his horse.

1868 Riots break out in Blaenafon during the General Election.
The LNWR line is opened between Blaenafon and Brynmawr.
Death of Thomas Hill the third.

1870 Elementary Education is made compulsory for all children.
Truck system is banned by Parliament.

1872 Crawshay Bailey restores Llanfoist Church.

1873 The Blaenafon Company are operating 16 collieries in addition to the ironworks.

1877 Death of John Frost.
Sydney Gilchrist Thomas and Percy Gilchrist carry out experiments at the Blaenafon works to reduce the phosphorus content of steel.

1879 Blaenafon Ironworks Company is reformed and the name is shortened to Blaenafon Company Ltd., with a new board of directors.

1880 Blaenafon Ironworks is rated as the most modern in the world.
Andrew Carnegie an American ironmaster pays 25,000 dollars for the Gilchrist Thomas formula.
The shaft at Kearsleys pit is deepened and the mine becomes known as Big Pit.
Great Western Railway take over the stock of the Monmouthshire Railway and Canal company.

"Iron accommodates itself to all our wants, our desires, and even our caprices; it is equally serviceable to the arts, the sciences, to agriculture, and war; the same ore furnishes the sword, the ploughshare, the spring of a watch or of a carriage, the chisel, the chain, the anchor, the compass, the cannon, and the bomb. It is a medicine of much virtue, and the only metal friendly to the human frame." Dr. Ure 1841.

MUSEUMS

The Valley Inheritance
Pontypool Park Buildings, Pontypool, Gwent.
Off A4043 at Town Bridge entrance to Pontypool Park.
Tel: Pontypool (04955) 52043.
Open: All year Monday to Saturday 10 am to 5 pm. Sunday 2 pm — 5 pm.

Canal Exhibition Centre.
Junction Cottage, Pontymoile, Pontypool, Gwent.
A canal toll keeper's cottage just off A4051 — access off Fountain Road to the south of Pontypool. Tel: Pontypool (04955) 52036 for information on opening hours.

Fourteen Locks Canal Interpretation Centre, near Newport.
High Cross, Rogerstone, Newport — just off M4 at junction 27.
Open Easter to September (not Tuesdays or Wednesdays) 10.30 am — 5pm.

Newport Museum.
John Frost Square, Newport.
Open: Monday to Saturday 10 am — 5.30 pm.

Big Pit Mining Museum, Blaenafon.
See page 73 for details.
Open: Daily, May to September, Monday to Saturday 10 am — 5 pm.
    Sunday 2 pm — 5 pm. For details of Winter opening tel: (0495) 790311.

Blaenafon Ironworks.
North Street, Blaenfon.
Details of the opening arrangements and guided tours may be obtained from the Valley Inheritance Centre at Pontypool. (See above).

SUGGESTED READING

Cordell. A.
Rape of the Fair Country,
Victor Gollancz 1959, Coronet Books.

Davies. E.J.
The Blaenavon Story,
Torfaen Council 1975.

Davies. T.G.
Blaenavon and Sydney Gilchrist Thomas,
Historical Metallurgy Society 1978.

Hadfield. H.
The Canals of South Wales and the Border,
David and Charles 1967.

Rattenbury. G.
Tramroads of the Brecknock and Abergavenny Canal,
Railway and Canal Historical Society 1980.

Rees, D. Morgan.
Mines Mills and Furnaces,
H.M.S.O. 1969.

Scrivenor. H.
Comprehensive History of the Iron Trade,
London 1841.

van Laun. J.
The Clydach Gorge,
Brecon Beacons National Park Committee 1979.

van Laun. J.
Pattern of Past Industry,
Brecon Beacons National Park Committee 1976.

OTHER TITLES BY CHRIS BARBER.
Walks in the Brecon Beacons, Pridgeon 1976. (Out of print).
Exploring the Waterfall Country, Pridgeon 1976. (Out of print).
Ghosts of Wales, John Jones, Cardiff 1979. (Out of print).
Exploring the Brecon Beacons National Park, Regional Publications 1980/85.
Exploring Gwent, Regional Publications 1984.
Mysterious Wales, David & Charles (hardback) 1982, Granada (Paladin Paperback) 1983.